Contents

BPP LEARNING MEDIA

Introduction to the course

Syllabus overview

This unit covers the skills and knowledge that you need in order to be able to identify the movements of cash within the business and make informed decisions on the best course of action to maximise the wealth of the business.

This unit provides a link to the importance of cash management to a business. It is generally accepted that a large number of organisations fail not through a lack of generated sales orders but through an inability to make sound financial decisions in controlling cash and working capital, and making informed decisions in investing surplus funds or raising cash when need dictates. Those organisations that manage their cash resources effectively have a lower risk of failure than those where these controls show signs of a severe lack of robustness and scrutiny on critical decisions that ensure the buoyancy of cash within the business.

Accounting technicians may be required to provide management with information that will aid them in making informed executive decisions to control spending, raise finance if and when needed, invest surplus funds and maximise the return on those funds in accordance with risk management. You will learn to be able to identify non-cash items in the financial information provided and eliminate these using techniques that will monitor the flow of cash into and out of the business.

This unit will provide you not only with an understanding of the theoretical principles of effective cash management but also with the practical skills needed to identify the various options available and to make informed decisions on the most viable course of action.

Cash and Treasury Management is an **optional** unit.

Test specification for this unit assessment

Assessment method	Marking type	Duration of assessment
Computer based assessment	Partially computer / partially human marked	2.5 hours

Learning outcomes	Weighting
1 Use statistical techniques and financial information to prepare forecasts of cash receipts and payments	10%
2 Prepare cash budgets and monitor cash flows within the organisation	20%
3 Evaluate the principles of cash management within the context of regulation and government monetary policies	20%
4 Evaluate ways of raising finance in accordance with organisational requirements	25%
5 Evaluate ways of investing surplus funds within organisational policies	25%
Total	**100%**

Assessment structure

2½ hours duration

Competency is 70%

*Note that this is only a guideline as to what might come up. The format and content of each task may vary from what we have listed below.

In any one assessment, you may not be assessed on all content, or on the full depth or breadth of a piece of content. The content assessed may change over time to ensure validity of assessment, but all assessment criteria will be tested over time.

The task structure below is estimated from the first sample assessment available from AAT. As each assessment doesn't test everything, further estimates have been made as to where some content could be assessed. It is, therefore, subject to change as more information becomes available.

Task	Expected content	Max marks	Chapter ref	Study complete
Task 1	**Identify cash receipts and payments and reconcile cash to profit** Identify and classify different types of cash receipts and payments Reconcile profit with movement in cash	8	1,3	
Task 2	**Prepare forecasts and calculate prices**	8	2	
Task 3	**Prepare cash budgets and use them** Prepare cash budgets and/or forecasts in the preferred format and clearly indicate net cash requirements, including the effects of lagged receipts Calculate non-current assets cash movements Undertake sensitivity analysis on cash budgets and make recommendations to management	10	3,4	
Task 4	**Forecast payables and receivables**	10	2	

Task	Expected content	Max marks	Chapter ref	Study complete
Task 5	**Compare cash budgets to plan and recommend action** Identify deviations from the cash budget and recommend corrective action within organisational policies	12	5	
Task 6	**Evaluate the principles of cash management within the context of regulation and government monetary policies** Explain how government monetary policies affect an organisation's treasury functions Discuss the principles of liquidity management Discuss how an organisation's principles of cash management will be determined by their specific financial regulations, guidelines and security procedures Discuss the role of the treasury function	32	6,8	
Task 7	**Raising finance – available alternatives** Demonstrate an understanding of how an organisation can raise finance and the basic terms and conditions associated with each of these types of financing	22	7	
Task 8	**Raising finance – evaluate terms** Evaluate the use of financing options to fund the organisation's cash requirements on the most beneficial terms and conditions	18	7	

Task	Expected content	Max marks	Chapter ref	Study complete
Task 9	**Surplus funds: alternative sources and impact of economic conditions** Evaluate different types of investment and the associated risk, terms and conditions Evaluate economic conditions that could affect various financial markets	22	8	
Task 10	**Surplus funds: Risk and organisational policy** Analyse ways to manage risk when investing to minimise potential exposure to the organisation Consider the investment of surplus funds according to organisational culture and policy	18	8	

Skills bank

Our experience of preparing students for this type of assessment suggests that to obtain competency, you will need to develop a number of key skills.

What do I need to know to do well in the assessment?

This unit is one of the optional Level 4 units.

To be successful in the assessment you need to:

- Understand the fundamental decisions and basic thinking behind different cash and treasury techniques including investing surplus cash balances and raising finance. These requirements will often be tested in narrative questions.

- Apply the techniques to 'real life' situations. These will often be tested in numerical questions, but you will also have to demonstrate your understanding of key data, such as using information for forecasting cash receipts and payments including monitoring cash flows in an organisation.

Assumed knowledge

Cash and Treasury Management is an **optional** unit and covers concepts that may be new to you. However, the unit builds on the fundamental concepts and techniques introduced at the Foundation Certificate and Advanced Diploma levels, as well as linking with other Professional Diploma units such as *Management Accounting: Decision and Control*.

Assessment style

In the assessment you will complete tasks by:

1   Entering narrative by selecting from drop down menus of narrative options known as **picklists**

2   Using **drag and drop** menus to enter narrative

3   Typing in numbers, known as **gapfill** entry

4   Entering **ticks**

5   Entering **dates** by selecting from a calendar

6   **Written** answers

You must familiarise yourself with the style of the online questions and the AAT software before taking the assessment. As part of your revision, login to the **AAT website** and attempt their **online practice assessments**.

Answering written questions

In your assessment there will be written questions on cash and treasury management and topics will include investment decisions and decisions to be made when raising finance. The main verbs used for these type of question requirements are as follows, along with their meaning:

- Identify – Analyse and select for presentation
- Explain – Set out in detail the meaning of
- Discuss – By argument, discuss the pros and cons

Analysing the scenario

Before answering the question set, you need to carefully review the scenario given in order to consider what questions need to be answered, and what needs to be discussed. A simple framework that could be used to answer the question is as follows:

- Point – make the point
- Evidence – use the information from the scenario as evidence
- Explain – explain why the evidence links to the point

For example, if an assessment task asks you to explain investment decision making, you could answer as follows:

1. Point – risk and return are important factors when making an investment decision

2. Evidence – investments in shares can provide dividends and capital growth however, they are perceived to have higher risk when compared to fixed rate investments

3. Explain – although returns can be high there is no guarantee of dividend payments and there is a possibility of capital loss due to market fluctuations

Recommendations are normally also required and a recommendation should provide guidance on how to proceed:

Recommendation – as the directors are risk-adverse an investment in shares should not be selected as an investment for surplus funds

The above approach provides a formula or framework that can be followed to answer written questions.

Introduction to the assessment

The question practice you do will prepare you for the format of tasks you will see in the *Cash and Treasury Management* assessment. It is also useful to familiarise yourself with the introductory information you **may** be given at the start of the assessment. For example:

You have **2 hours and 30 minutes** to complete this sample assessment.

The assessment contains **10 tasks** and you should attempt to complete **every** task.

Each task is independent. You will not need to refer to your answers to previous tasks.

Read every task carefully to make sure you understand what is required.

Where the date is relevant, it is given in the task data.

Both minus signs and brackets can be used to indicate negative numbers **unless** task instructions say otherwise.

You must use a full stop to indicate a decimal point. For example, write 100.57 NOT 100,57 OR 100 57.

You may use a comma to indicate a number in the thousands, but you don't have to. For example, 10000 and 10,000 are both acceptable.

---

1   As you revise, use the **BPP Passcards** to consolidate your knowledge. They are a pocket-sized revision tool, perfect for packing in that last-minute revision.

2   Attempt as many tasks as possible in the **Question Bank**. There are plenty of assessment-style tasks which are excellent preparation for the real assessment.

3   Always **check** through your own answers as you will in the real assessment, before looking at the solutions in the back of the Question Bank.

Key to icons

Key term — A key definition which is important to be aware of for the assessment

Formula to learn — A formula you will need to learn as it will not be provided in the assessment

Formula provided — A formula which is provided within the assessment and generally available as a pop-up on screen

Activity — An example which allows you to apply your knowledge to the technique covered in the Course Book. The solution is provided at the end of the chapter

Illustration — A worked example which can be used to review and see how an assessment question could be answered

Assessment focus point — A high priority point for the assessment

Open book reference — Where use of an open book will be allowed for the assessment

Real life examples — A practical real life scenario

AAT qualifications

The material in this book may support the following AAT qualifications:

AAT Professional Diploma in Accounting Level 4, AAT Professional Diploma in Accounting at SCQF Level 8 and Certificate: Accounting (Level 5 AATSA).

Supplements

From time to time we may need to publish supplementary materials to one of our titles. This can be for a variety of reasons, from a small change in the AAT unit guidance to new legislation coming into effect between editions.

You should check our supplements page regularly for anything that may affect your learning materials. All supplements are available free of charge on our supplements page on our website at:

www.bpp.com/learning-media/about/students

Improving material and removing errors

There is a constant need to update and enhance our study materials in line with both regulatory changes and new insights into the assessments.

From our team of authors BPP appoints a subject expert to update and improve these materials for each new edition.

Their updated draft is subsequently technically checked by another author and from time to time non-technically checked by a proof reader.

We are very keen to remove as many numerical errors and narrative typos as we can but given the volume of detailed information being changed in a short space of time we know that a few errors will sometimes get through our net.

We apologise in advance for any inconvenience that an error might cause. We continue to look for new ways to improve these study materials and would welcome your suggestions. Please feel free to contact our AAT Head of Programme at nisarahmed@bpp.com if you have any suggestions for us.

Cash flow and profit

1

Learning outcomes

1.2	Reconcile profit with movement in cash
	Students need to be able to
	• Reconcile the differences between other payables accounting and cash accounting, including:
	– Adjusting for non-cash items
	– Taking accounts to opening and closing balances in the financial statements and/or bank statements
	– Calculating movements in cash
1.4	Calculate non-current assets cash movements
	Students need to be able to
	• Calculate the following:
	– The purchase price of the non-current asset
	– The sale price of the non-current asset
	– The carrying value of the non-current asset, including revaluation
	– The effect of revaluation on cash on the disposal of a non-current asset

Assessment context

You need to be able to calculate actual business cash receipts and cash payments from a profit or loss account, and statement of financial position (SOFP) information.

Qualification context

The distinction between cash and profit is a fundamental concept that you need to fully understand throughout your accounting career.

Business context

Cash flow is the life blood of any business; without proper financial management, even solid, profitable business ideas run the risk of failure.

Chapter overview

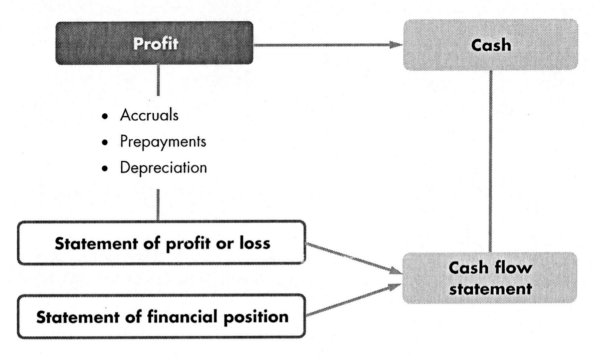

- Accruals
- Prepayments
- Depreciation

- Receivables
- Payables
- Non-current assets

Introduction

This chapter is designed to enable you to distinguish between cash and profit.

The aim of most businesses is to make a **profit** for its owners. If a business is profitable, this means that it is making more by selling its goods or services than it is spending on the purchase of goods and the payment of expenses.

Profit is **not** the same as cash. A profitable business may still fail if it cannot pay its bills.

1 Cash flow versus profit

Cash is ready money, most easily thought of as banknotes and coins, and money in a current bank account. It has been described many times as the lifeblood of business in a modern economy.

Activity 1: Differences between cash flow and profit

Required

Give four reasons why profits and cash differ.

Solution

(a)

(b)

(c)

(d)

2 Deriving cash flow information from the statement of profit or loss

It is possible to calculate the value of **cash transactions** by adjusting figures in the statement of profit or loss to reverse the effect of accounting adjustments such as accruals, prepayments and depreciation.

Budgeted statement of profit or loss   **Cash budget**

Figures based on **accruals concept** ———→ Figures based on when cash is received or paid

Sales ————————————————————→ Receipts from sales

Cost of sales ———————————————→ Payments for purchases

Expenses ————————————————→ Payments for expenses

2.1 The accruals concept

In the statement of profit or loss, revenue from sales and the cost of goods and expenses are accounted for in the period in which they are earned or incurred, rather than in the period in which the cash is received or paid.

2.2 Non-cash expenses

Depreciation charge or a **loss on the sale of a non-current asset** appear in the statement of profit or loss but are **non-cash expenses**. They must be added back to show the cash position.

A **provision** for an expense in the future is also a non-cash expense which needs to be added back.

2.3 Deriving cash flow from the statement of financial position

Cash flow will also be affected by changes in working capital – inventory, receivables and payables. The relevant figures come from comparison of the opening and closing budgeted balance sheets (statement of financial position).

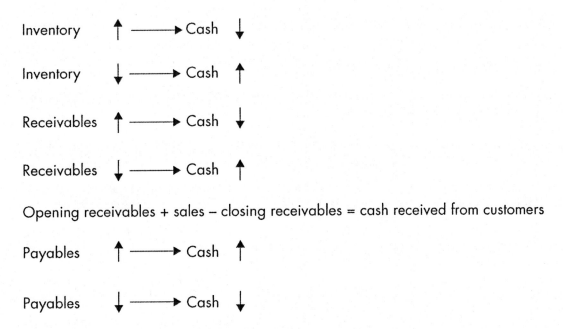

Inventory ↑ ——→ Cash ↓

Inventory ↓ ——→ Cash ↑

Receivables ↑ ——→ Cash ↓

Receivables ↓ ——→ Cash ↑

Opening receivables + sales – closing receivables = cash received from customers

Payables ↑ ——→ Cash ↑

Payables ↓ ——→ Cash ↓

Opening payables + purchases – closing payables = cash paid to suppliers

Now that we understand the difference between profit and cash, and the impact of **credit transactions**, we can use the financial statements to derive cash flow information.

Illustration 1: Deriving cashflow from financial statements

SC Fuel and Glass Ltd has a small lubricants division known as SCL. The budgeted statement of profit or loss for the three months ending 31 December is given below for SCL.

Budgeted statement of profit or loss – three months ending 31 December

	£000	£000
Revenue		840
Cost of sales		
Opening inventory	31	
Purchases	588	
	619	
Less closing inventory	(47)	
		(572)
Gross profit		268
Other operating costs		(130)
Profit from operations		138

The figure for other operating costs includes £24,000 of depreciation charges and an estimated profit of £3,000 on the sale of a non-current asset that is expected to realise £20,000 during the period.

The budgeted statements of financial position for SCL at 30 September and 31 December are as follows:

Budgeted statements of financial position

	31 December		30 September	
	£000	£000	£000	£000
Non-current assets		948		809
Current assets:				
Inventory	47		31	
Receivables	50		62	
Prepayments for other				
operating costs	8		4	
	105		97	
Current liabilities:				
Trade payables	41		35	
Bank overdraft	3		–	
	44		35	
Net current assets		61		62
		1,009		871
Equity		500		500
Retained earnings		509		371
		1,009		871

From the budgeted statement of profit or loss and the budgeted statements of financial position, we will now prepare the budgeted cash flows for sales, purchases and other operating costs.

Cash inflow from sales

The figure for revenue is £840,000. However, there were opening trade receivables of £62,000 and closing trade receivables of £50,000. This means that the actual cash flow from sales was £840,000 + £62,000 − £50,000 = £852,000. The reasoning for this is that the amount of sales actually made during the period was £840,000 but of this, £50,000 remains uncollected at the end of the period. In addition, the opening trade receivables of £62,000 would have been received during the period.

Cash outflow for purchases

The figure for purchases in the statement of profit or loss is £588,000 (note that we need the purchases figure, not the cost of sales figure). Of these purchases, £41,000 were still not paid (being the closing trade payables figure) whereas the opening trade payables of £35,000 would have been paid. Therefore, the cash flow for purchases for the period would be £588,000 + £35,000 − £41,000 = £582,000.

Depreciation

This is not a cash expense, therefore there would be no cash flow for the period.

Sale of non-current asset

The profit figure for the sale of the non-current asset is not a cash flow, simply a book entry to reflect the difference between the carrying value of the non-current asset and the cash proceeds. However, the anticipated sales proceeds of £20,000 are a budgeted cash inflow.

Cash payment for overheads

The charge for other operating costs in total is £130,000 but this includes two non-cash items – a profit on sale of a non-current asset of £3,000 and depreciation of £24,000. Therefore, we need to remove the depreciation and add back the profit on sale so the cash based overheads are £130,000 − £24,000 + £3,000 = £109,000.

However, from the statement of financial position, we can see that there are also opening prepayments of £4,000 and closing prepayments of £8,000. The opening prepayment figure of £4,000 has already been paid but the closing prepayment figure of £8,000 will be paid during the period. Therefore, the estimated cash flow for overheads is £109,000 − £4,000 + £8,000 = £113,000.

Activity 2: Cash flow from statement of profit or loss and statement of financial position

Given below is the forecast statement of profit or loss for a company for next year ending 31 December 20X4.

Forecast statement of profit or loss for year ending 31 December 20X4

	£000
Sales revenue	2,000
Cost of sales	(1,500)
Gross profit	500
Other operating expenses	(150)
Profit from operations	350
Tax	(70)
Profit after tax	280

Additional information

(i)   Other operating expenses include the following:

- An accrual for an expected electricity bill of £1,500 which will arrive after the year end

- A depreciation charge of £50,000

- A loss on the sale of a lorry of £1,700 with all other expenses being settled on cash terms

(ii)   At the end of the year, a rent payment of £3,500 will be paid in advance.

(iii) The company held inventory of £12,000, payables of £11,000 and receivables of £15,000 at the start of the year. At the end of the year, inventory was £21,000, payables were £14,000, and receivables were £24,000.

(iv)   The tax payable shown in the statement of financial position is expected to be £65,000 at 1 January 20X4; and £75,000 at 31 December 20X4.

(v)   The carrying value of non-current assets at 1 January 20X4 is forecast to be £300,000; and £280,000 at 31 December 20X4. Any additions to non-current assets during the year will be paid in cash immediately.

(vi)   The forecast cash balance as at 1 January 20X4 is £5,000 in overdraft.

Required

Use the table below to forecast the closing cash position at 31 December 20X4.

Use minus signs for negative values where appropriate and insert a 0 if no adjustment is required.

Solution

	Working	£
Profit from operations		
Change in inventory		
Change in trade receivables		
Change in trade payables		
Rent prepayment		
Electricity accrual		
Depreciation charge		
Loss on sale of lorry		
Tax paid		
Purchase of non-current assets		
NET change in cash position		
Forecast cash position on 1 January 20X4		
Forecast cash position on 31 December 20X4		

Assessment focus point

In your assessment you could be asked to calculate cash flows from a variety of basic information. Remember in principle to consider:

- The **opening balance on the statement of financial position**; add

- The income or expense for the period in the **statement of profit or loss**; less

- The **closing balance on the statement of financial position**.

Activity 3: Benje

Benje prepares a quarterly income statement and statement of financial position. The following information has been extracted for the last quarter:

Extract from statement of profit or loss for quarter ended 31 December

	£
Sales	72,960
Less purchases	(10,944)
Gross profit	62,016

Extract from the statement of financial position as at 1 October and 31 December

	1 October £	31 December £
Receivables	8,648	6,560
Payables	304	450

Required

Calculate the actual business cash receipts and cash payments for the quarter to 31 December and complete the table below:

Solution

	Workings	£
Sales receipts		
Purchases payments		

2.4 Calculating cash received on disposal of non-current assets

If a non-current asset is disposed of, and information is given about its carrying amount and the profit or loss on disposal, it is possible to find the amount of cash received for the asset.

Illustration 2: Non-current assets

A business has an opening balance for non-current assets in the statement of financial position of £100,000 and a closing balance of £120,000. The statement of profit or loss shows a £10,000 charge for depreciation during the period.

The amount of cash spent on additional non-current assets is:

	£
Opening balance	100,000
Less depreciation charge	(10,000)
	90,000
Closing balance	120,000
Cash expenditure	30,000

The logic for this is that the balance for non-current assets has increased by £20,000 in the statement of financial position but this is after charging £10,000 of depreciation. Therefore, in order to have increased this much, there must have been £30,000 of new expenditure on non-current assets.

Note. This assumed that no non-current assets were sold in the period.

Activity 4: Cash on disposal of non-current assets

A business decides to sell one of its buildings which originally cost £105,000. At the date of disposal, accumulated depreciation on the building amounted to £48,500. The sale generated a profit on disposal of £35,000.

Required

What were the cash proceeds on disposal of the building?

	✓
£21,500	
£56,500	
£70,000	
£91,500	

Chapter summary

- As a starting point for this unit, it is important to realise how vital cash is to a business, even if the business is profitable, as it must be able to meet its payments as and when they fall due.

- There are a number of differences between profit and cash due to the accruals concept, non-cash expenses, receipts or payments which do not affect profit, purchases and sales of non-current assets.

- Cash transactions are where a form of money is received or paid immediately, whereas in a credit transaction, goods are received or sent immediately but payment is delayed by agreement between the buyer and the seller.

- Budgeted statement of profit or loss figures for sales revenue, purchases, expenses etc can be used, when combined with accounting adjustments such as accruals, prepayments and depreciation charges, to find the budgeted cash flow figures for the period.

- Expenditure on non-current assets may also need to be derived from the statement of financial position figures for non-current assets; and the depreciation charge, in the statement of profit or loss.

- Information may be presented in the form of ledger accounts. Opening and closing ledger account balances, and the income or expense figure from the statement of profit or loss, may be used to determine the cash received or paid for a period.

- The net movement in cash for a period can be derived from the statement of profit or loss, and statement of financial position and supporting information.

- A business will have different types of cash transactions. Cash flows may be regular, irregular, exceptional, capital or revenue, variable or fixed.

Keywords

- **Accruals concept:** Revenue and expenses are accounted for in the period in which they are incurred, rather than the period in which the cash is received or paid

- **Cash budget:** A detailed budget of estimated cash inflows and outflows

- **Cash transaction:** A transaction by cash, cheque, credit card or debit card

- **Credit transaction:** A transaction where receipt or payment of cash is delayed for a period of time

- **Depreciation charge:** An accounting expense spreading the depreciable amount (initial cost – scrap value) of a non-current asset over the period of ownership

- **Non-cash expenses:** Expenses of the business which are charged to profit but do not affect the amount of cash in the business, for example, depreciation of a non-current asset

1 **Selecting from the picklists, complete the following sentence:**

Although it is important for a business to [make a profit/have a healthy cash balance], it can be argued that it is even more important for a business to [make a profit/have a healthy cash balance] in order to be able to pay amounts when they are due.

2 **Which of the following are factors that account for the difference between the amount of profit a business makes and its cash balance? Tick the relevant reasons:**

	✓
Prepayment of rent	
Purchase of a non-current asset	
Purchases of inventory for cash	
Depreciation	
Cash sales	

3 A company has opening non-current assets with a carrying value of £275,000. During the year, depreciation of £17,250 was charged to the statement of profit or loss. At the end of the year, the carrying value of non-current assets was £305,000.

What was the cash paid to acquire non-current assets during the year?

4 At the start of the year, a company owns a machine which originally cost £55,000 and on which accumulated depreciation is £32,500. During the year, the machine is sold, giving rise to a loss on disposal of £3,750. The company has a policy of not charging depreciation on non-current assets in the year of disposal.

What cash proceeds were received on disposal of the machine?

5   Given below is the forecast statement of profit or loss for a company for the three months ending 31 December, together with forecast statements of financial position at 30 September and 31 December.

Forecast statement of profit or loss for three months ending 31 December

	£000	£000
Sales revenue		720
Opening inventory	78	
Purchases	471	
Less closing inventory	(81)	
Cost of sales		(468)
Gross profit		252
Other operating costs		(130)
Profit from operations		122

Included in the figure for other operating costs is £64,000 of depreciation charge for the year.

Forecast statements of financial position

	31 December £000	£000	30 September £000	£000
Non-current assets		584		426
Current assets:				
Inventories	81		78	
Trade receivables	75		60	
Cash	–		12	
	156		150	
Current liabilities:				
Trade payables	104		70	
Accruals	13		5	
	117		75	
Net current assets		39		75
		623		501

	31 December		30 September	
	£000	£000	£000	£000
Equity		400		400
Retained earnings		223		101
		623		501

From the forecast statement of profit or loss and forecast statements of financial position, calculate the following cash flow figures for the three months ending 31 December.

	£
Sales receipts	
Purchases payments	
Expenses payments	
Depreciation	

6 The following information has been extracted from the purchases ledger control account for the year ended 31 December:

	£
Opening trade payables	24,530
Closing trade payables	17,967
Purchases per statement of profit or loss	253,364

Complete the entries in the control account to determine the cash paid to suppliers during the year:

Purchases ledger control account

	Debit £		Credit £	
Cash paid (β)				

7 The following information relates to the insurance expense account for June:

	£
Opening accrual	4,530
Closing accrual	3,797
Insurance expense per statement of profit or loss	13,364

Complete the expense account to determine the cash paid for insurance during the year:

Insurance expense account

	Debit £		Credit £
Cash paid (β)			

Forecasting income and expenditure

2

Learning outcomes

1.3	Prepare forecasts
	Students need to be able to
	• Calculate the following:
	– Mark-up
	– Margin
	– Moving averages
	– Percentages
	– Regression analysis
	– Trends
	– Seasonal variations
	– Index numbers

Assessment context

You need to be able to forecast sales, purchases and expenses information.

Qualification context

You will cover forecasting in other Level 4 papers, *Management Accounting: Budgeting* and *Management Accounting: Decision and Control*.

Business context

Businesses will use a variety of models and techniques to help them forecast the performance of their business.

Chapter overview

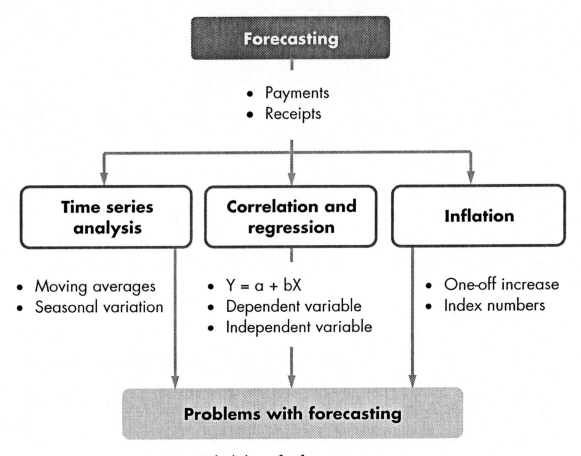

Forecasting

- Payments
- Receipts

Time series analysis

- Moving averages
- Seasonal variation

Correlation and regression

- $Y = a + bX$
- Dependent variable
- Independent variable

Inflation

- One-off increase
- Index numbers

Problems with forecasting

- Reliability of information
- Assumes past trends will continue in the future

Introduction

In order to prepare cash budgets, forecasts of payments and receipts will need to be undertaken. There are various statistical techniques which can be used.

1 Trend analysis

A **time series** is a series of actual figures or values recorded over time.

Examples – Output at a factory each day for the last month
– Total costs per annum for last ten years
– Monthly sales over last five years

An analysis of past patterns of these figures can be used to **extrapolate** or estimate expected patterns in the future.

We can draw a graph of the data and use the trend line to forecast future sales. For example:

Sales (units)

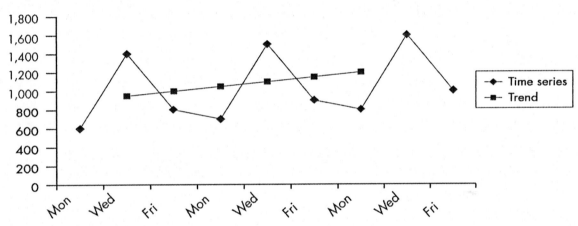

The trend line could then be extended to form a forecast line.

Activity 1: Trend analysis

Sam wants to produce a forecast of sales and has recorded the following recent sales figures (in units).

January	5,000
February	5,200
March	5,800
April	6,300
May	6,900
June	7,200

Required

What is the average monthly change in sales? [   ] **units**

What would be the forecast sales for July? [   ] **units**

Workings (not provided in CBT)

---

2 Time series analysis

Key term

Trend (T) The underlying increase or decrease in demand.

For example, a steady decline in the average sales of a national daily newspaper or a steady increase in sales of Sony PlayStations.

Moving averages and regression analysis can be used to calculate the trend.

If seasonal variations repeat after four periods, say, we can smooth out these variations, and calculate the underlying trend, by looking at averages for each quarter's figures.

Seasonal variations (SV) Short-term repeated fluctuations from the trend.

For example, sales of tabloid newspapers are higher on Mondays and Saturdays than other days due to the extra sports coverage, or sales of ice cream being higher in summer than in winter.

Cyclical variations Recurring patterns over a longer period of time, not generally of a fixed nature. Hence for practical purposes, they are ignored in the analysis.

For example, changes in unemployment, movement from recession to economic growth.

Random variations Variations due to unexplained or random events so these will be included in past data but would not be included in future estimates.

For example, fall in sales due to floods, earthquakes, war, etc.

2.1 Linear regression

Regression analysis (also known as the '**line of best fit**') establishes the relationship between two sets of data and finds mathematically the straight line using all pairs of data that 'fits' best through the data.

The linear (straight line) relationship between the two variables can be determined using the equation of a straight line, $Y = a + bX$.

Both a and b are constants and represent specific figures, whereas X is the independent variable, and Y is the dependent variable.

For example, sales is dependent (variable Y) of advertising expenditure (independent variable X).

Assessment focus point

In your assessment you will **not** have to calculate values of **a** and **b** from raw data in the regression equation $y = a + bx$. However, you may have to use the equation to forecast sales and costs.

Activity 2: Regression line

The operations director of a food manufacturer has provided you with the regression equation and information to estimate the price per litre of virgin oil for the next three months.

The equation is $Y = a + bX$ where:

X is the time period in months

Y is the price of the oil in £

The value of X for October 20X4 is 10

The constant 'a' is 1.998 and the constant 'b' is 0.006

Required

Establish the regression line and calculate the expected price of the oil for November 20X4, December 20X4 and January 20X5 (to 3 decimal places).

The regression line is _____

The expected price of the oil for November 20X4 is £ ☐

The expected price of the oil for December 20X4 is £ ☐

The expected price of the oil for January 20X5 is £ ☐

2.2 Moving averages

The main method for calculating a trend from a time series is the technique of **moving averages**, which is an average of the results of a fixed number of periods and relates to the mid-point of the overall period.

A moving average can be taken using either an even or an odd number of figures for each average. Both methods are examinable under this syllabus.

The period over which a moving average should be calculated is dependent on the nature of the time series. The most suitable moving average is one which covers a full cycle. For example, the sales every week from Monday to Friday ie five-day average would be an odd period moving average (as seen in the worked example below).

2.2.1 Centred moving average

If moving averages are taken of results in an even number of time periods, while the basic technique is the same, the mid-point would not relate to a specific time period.

If an average was taken of four months, the average would relate to the mid-point of these periods, between months 2 and 3. In this case, in order to find the trend, there is a further calculation to make, the **centred moving average**.

Illustration 1: Moving averages

The sales figures for the fuel division of SC Fuel and Glass for the last year are as follows:

Time period	Sales £000
January	2,030
February	1,570
March	1,620
April	2,100
May	2,080
June	1,740
July	1,690
August	2,190
September	2,150
October	1,830
November	1,780
December	2,200

Start with the total of the first four months' sales, January to April:

2,030 + 1,570 + 1,620 + 2,100 = 7,320

The average of this is 7,320/4 = 1,830 (written in the table between February and March).

Repeat for the next four months, February to May, whose total is 7,370 and average is 1,842 (written between March and April).

The centred moving average is then calculated by taking each consecutive pair of four-month moving average figures and, in turn, averaging them:

First centred moving average = (1,830 + 1,842)/2 = 1,836 (written against March) and so on.

Time period	Sales £000	Moving total 4 months' sales £000	Moving average 4 months' sales £000	Centred moving average £000
January	2,030			
February	1,570			
		7,320	1,830	
March	1,620			1,836
		7,370	1,842	
April	2,100			1,864
		7,540	1,885	
May	2,080			1,894
		7,610	1,903	
June	1,740			1,914
		7,700	1,925	
July	1,690			1,934
		7,770	1,943	
August	2,190			1,954
		7,860	1,965	
September	2,150			1,977
		7,950	1,988	
October	1,830			1,989
		7,960	1,990	
November	1,780			
December	2,200			

The trend can then be estimated from the centred moving averages. The moving average goes from 1,836 in March to 1,989 in October, during which time, there are a total of 7 increases.

We can therefore see that the trend for the sales figures shows an average increase in each month of about £22,000 ((1,989 – 1,836)/7 changes in trend = £21,857).

A centred moving average might be appropriate if, for example, the data was given in the form of quarterly sales figures, with four sets of data making up a year.

2.3 The additive model and the multiplicative model

A time series model is based on the assumption that seasonal variations are either fixed amounts (additive) or constant proportions of the trend (multiplicative).

In the **additive model**, the components are assumed to add together to give the time series.

Formula to learn

In the additive model, the components are assumed to add together to give the time series:

TS = T + SV

Whereas in the **multiplicative model**, the components are multiplied together to give the time series:

TS = T × SV

2.4 Calculation of the seasonal variation

The models are then used to calculate the seasonal variation by rearranging the time series equations above.

Formula to learn

Additive model: SV = TS – T

Multiplicative model: SV = TS/T

Activity 3: Time series – additive model

Felicity Publications has decided to make the most of the rapidly growing magazine market by launching a new magazine dedicated to celebrity gossip. The new magazine is to be sold three times a week. Sales data has been collected for the magazine's initial launch period.

Time period		Time series (sales)
Week 1	Mon	600
	Wed	1,380
	Fri	810
Week 2	Mon	690
	Wed	1,470
	Fri	900
Week 3	Mon	780
	Wed	1,560
	Fri	990

Required

(a) Use moving averages to find the trend and to forecast daily sales in Week 4.

(b) If each magazine is to be sold at a price of £1.50, what figure for sales receipts would go in the Week 4 cash budget?

Solution

(a)

Week	Day	Time series (TS)	Moving average (T)	Seasonal variation (SV)
1	Mon	600		
	Wed	1,380		
	Fri	810		
2	Mon	690		
	Wed	1,470		
	Fri	900		
3	Mon	780		
	Wed	1,560		
	Fri	990		

Average change in trend =

Forecast sales

		Forecast trend	SV	Forecast sales
Week 3	Fri			
Week 4	Mon			
	Wed			
	Fri			

(b)   Total sales receipts for week 4 = £ ☐

Assessment focus point

In your assessment, make sure that you deduct a negative seasonal variation from the trend, or add a positive seasonal variation.

Activity 4: Time series – multiplicative model

The trend figures for a business's quarterly sales are given below, together with the seasonal variations using the multiplicative model.

The seasonal variations have been calculated as follows:

Quarter	Q1	Q2	Q3	Q4
SV	0.97	1.39	0.64	1.00

Required

Use this information to determine the estimated sales figures for the four quarters of 20X4.

Solution

20X4	Forecast trend £	Seasonal variation %	Forecast sales £
Q1	490,300		
Q2	496,100		
Q3	501,900		
Q4	507,700		

2.5 Problems with forecasting

The forecasting techniques we have covered are very useful but there are problems inherent in forecasting.

- The less historic data that is available, the less reliable will be the results.

- The further into the future we forecast, the less reliable will be the results.

- There is an assumption that the trend and seasonal variations from the past will continue into the future.

- Cyclical and random variations are ignored.

3 Inflation

Inflation is the increase in prices of goods and services over a period of time. In a cash budget, it may affect the values of:

- Selling prices
- Purchase prices
- Expenses
- Cost of non-current assets
- Labour costs

A business may have information about a **one-off increase** in sales price or an **annual increase** in the hourly rate paid to the workforce. These increases should be built into the cash budget.

Activity 5: Inflation

Edward is a manufacturer of teddy bears and is preparing the cash budget for the next three months. The selling price of the bears has been £20 per unit for some time and it has been decided to increase this price by 5% per unit every month from 1 February.

The workforce are currently paid at a rate of £7 per hour and each bear requires 3 hours of labour. From 1 March, there is to be a 2.5% increase in the hourly wage rate.

Sales and production for the three months of January to March are estimated as follows:

	Sales Bears	Production Bears
January	3,500	3,600
February	4,100	3,900
March	4,000	4,200

Required

What figures should be used in the cash budget for sales and for wages costs?

Solution

	Workings	£
Sales		
January		
February		
March		
Wages		
January		
February		
March		

4 Index numbers

A price index measures the change in value of an item or group of items over a period of time, compared to a defined **base** period.

An **index** is a measure of the changes over time in the price of an item or a group of items. Index numbers are normally expressed in terms of a **base year** or **base period** for which the value assigned to the index is 100. Any subsequent increases or decreases in the price of the item are then reflected in the value of the index.

4.1 Calculation of an index

The first step in the calculation of an index is to determine the base year and set the price in that year at a value of 100. The price in subsequent years is then expressed as a proportion of 100. If the price is higher than the base year price, the index will be greater than 100, but if it is lower than the base year price the index will be less than 100. The construction of an index may be required in the assessment.

Formula to learn

$$\text{Index} = \frac{\text{Current period's figure}}{\text{Base period figure}} \times 100$$

Illustration 2: Index calculation

The sales figures for a business for the first six months of the year are as follows:

	£
January	136,000
February	148,000
March	140,000
April	130,000
May	138,000
June	145,000

We will set the January figure as the base period, with an index of 100.

Each subsequent period's figure is converted to the equivalent index using the following formula:

$$\text{Index} = \frac{\text{Current period's figure}}{\text{Base period figure}} \times 100$$

The index for February is: $\dfrac{148{,}000}{136{,}000} \times 100 \quad = 109$

The index for March is: $\dfrac{140{,}000}{136{,}000} \times 100 \quad = 103$

The index for April is: $\dfrac{130{,}000}{136{,}000} \times 100 \quad = 96$

The index for May is: $\dfrac{138{,}000}{136{,}000} \times 100 \quad = 101$

The index for June is: $\dfrac{145{,}000}{136{,}000} \times 100 \quad = 107$

Activity 6: Index numbers

TeesRUs Ltd makes and packs tea bags. The tea is imported from India and the historical cost per kilogram is shown below.

Jun X7	Jul X7	Aug X7	Sep X7	Oct X7	Nov X7
£4.95	£4.97	£4.99	£5.05	£5.08	£5.10

Required

(a) **Convert the costs per kg for June and November into index numbers using January 20X7 as the base period. The price per kg at January 20X7 was £4.80.**

(b) **It is expected that the index number for tea in January 20X8 will be 108.25. Calculate the expected cost per kg for January 20X8.**

(c) **Calculate the percentage increase in the price of tea from January 20X7 to January 20X8.**

Solution

(a) Index number for June 20X7 is ☐ and November 20X7 is ☐

(b) Expected cost per kg of tea in January 20X8 is ☐

(c) Percentage increase in the price of tea from January 20X7 to January 20X8 is ☐

An index can either be a **Specific price index** (relating to one or a very limited range of items) or general – such as national inflation in a **General price index**.

The traditional method of measuring inflation in the UK has been the **Retail Price Index** (RPI), which compares the average cost of household expenditure to its equivalent cost in January 1987 (where 1987 is the base year). Unfortunately the RPI is not used consistently in all countries, so in January 2013 the UK Government switched to using the **Consumer Price Index** (CPI) to express inflation officially, although the RPI is still calculated. The CPI is used more generally internationally and measures the price increase of a slightly different basket of goods over time compared to the RPI. Both the CPI and the RPI attempt to measure general price increases in the economy.

When a business is preparing a forecast, there may not be any known specific increases in prices, but some expenses may be found to increase in line with the **general level of inflation** within the economy.

The inflated value of the cash flow can be found using this method:

Formula to learn

$$\text{Future cash flow} = \text{Current cash flow} \times \frac{\text{Future index}}{\text{Current index}}$$

Activity 7: Retail Price Index

Edward believes that overheads for his business increase in line with the general inflation rate, as indicated by the RPI. Overheads in December are £35,000 and the RPI is 154.8.

It is expected that the RPI will be 155.2 in January and 156.1 in February.

Required

What are the estimated overheads in January and February?

Solution

	Workings	Overheads £
January		
February		

5 Margins and mark-ups

A **margin** is the percentage of the final selling price that is profit.

With margins, the sale figure is always 100% and the margin is based on a percentage of sales.

A **mark-up** is the percentage of the cost price that is added on to get the selling price.

With mark-ups, the cost figure is always 100% and the mark-up is based on a percentage of the purchase cost.

Assessment focus point

In the **assessment**, you may have to use **margins** or **mark-ups** to forecast sales or purchases.

Activity 8: Mark-ups and margins

A retail business buys bags from a wholesaler, adds a mark-up of 40% on cost and then sells them to its customers, in the month of purchase, for cash.

The purchases are as follows:

	January £	February £	March £
Purchases	32,000	24,000	28,000

Required

(a) **Calculate the cash sales for each of January, February and March.**

(b) **If the mark-up on cost is 40%, then % margin on sales (to 0 dp) is _____%.**

Solution

(a)

	January £	February £	March £
Purchases			
Cash sales			

(b)

Chapter summary

- Cash budgets are based upon estimates of future cash inflows and outflows. In order to make a prediction about future behaviour, we can find relationships between variables (such as selling costs and sales volume) or look at past performance and assume that these patterns will continue in the future.

- Correlation is an expression of the relationship between two variables.

- We can use regression analysis to show the relationship between two variables as an equation in the form $Y = a + bX$.

- A time series is a series of historical figures over a period of time and the first stage in forecasting is to determine the trend of these figures using moving averages.

- A moving average is the average of each successive group of figures from a time series. Moving averages may be based on an odd or even number of figures. Where an even number of observations are used, a centred moving average must be calculated.

- Once the trend has been determined, the seasonal variations can be calculated, using either the additive model or the multiplicative model. In the assessment, either model can be tested.

- Once the trend and any seasonal variations are known, then this information can be used to estimate future figures by extrapolating the trend line into the future and applying the appropriate seasonal variation.

- In estimating future cash flows, account must be taken of any anticipated inflation. This may be in the form of a one-off specific price increase or a more general period by period increase.

- One method of expressing a change in prices is using an index. This could be a specific price index for a particular item of goods or services or a general price index such as the Retail Price Index (RPI) or Consumer Price Index (CPI).

- An index, with its associated future estimated value, can be used to convert a current cash flow value to its estimated actual future value.

- Margins or mark-ups can be used to forecast sales or purchases, given a production or sales plan.

- **Additive model:** A time series model where the actual figure is made up of the trend plus the seasonal variation

- **Base year/period:** The year or period upon which an index is based and to which the index value of 100 is assigned

- **Centred moving average:** When the moving average has been based on an even number of figures, the centred moving average is calculated by taking each consecutive pair of moving average figures and averaging them

- **Consumer Price Index:** A general index which measures changes in the cost of items of expenditure in the average household

- **Cyclical variations:** Long-term movements in a time series due to general economic conditions

- **Extrapolation:** Using historic data to make estimates of future figures

- **General price index:** A price index relating to a variety of goods and services

- **Index:** A measure of changes in price over time

- **Inflation:** The increase in prices of goods and services over time

- **Line of best fit:** A straight line drawn through a series of data points plotted on a scatter graph

- **Margin:** The percentage of the final selling price that is profit

- **Mark-up:** The percentage of the cost price that is added on to get the selling price

- **Moving average:** The average of each successive group of figures from a time series, used to determine the trend

- **Multiplicative model:** A time series model where each actual figure is expressed as a proportion of the trend. Sometimes called the proportional model

- **Random variations:** Variations in time series figures due to random or unexplained events

- **Regression analysis:** A statistical method of analysing the relationship between two variables, a dependent variable and an independent variable, also known as linear regression

- **Retail Price Index:** Another general index which measures the changes in the cost of items of expenditure in the average household. The assumed purchases (or 'basket of goods') differs from the Consumer Price Index. The Consumer Price Index is the official measure of general inflation in the UK

- **Seasonal variations (SV):** Variations of the figures for particular time periods from the trend due to seasonal factors

- **Specific price index:** A price index relating to a specific item of goods or services

- **Time series:** Any record of figures occurring over a past period

- **Time series analysis:** A method of analysing historic data in order to use the results for future calculations

- **Trend (T):** The general movement in a time series over time

1 Given below are the daily takings in a restaurant that is open five days a week, Tuesday to Saturday.

	Tue £	Wed £	Thu £	Fri £	Sat £
Week 1	560	600	630	880	930
Week 2	540	590	640	850	940
Week 3	550	560	600	870	970

Complete the table below to calculate the five day moving average of the daily takings.

		Takings £	5-day moving average £
Week 1	Tuesday		
	Wednesday		
	Thursday		
	Friday		
	Saturday		
Week 2	Tuesday		
	Wednesday		
	Thursday		
	Friday		
	Saturday		
Week 3	Tuesday		
	Wednesday		
	Thursday		
	Friday		
	Saturday		

2   Given below are the units produced in a factory from Monday to Friday for each day for three weeks.

	Mon Units	Tue Units	Wed Units	Thu Units	Fri Units
Week 1	1,400	1,600	1,800	1,800	1,550
Week 2	1,380	1,620	1,830	1,810	1,500
Week 3	1,450	1,650	1,850	1,840	1,570

(a) Complete the table below to calculate the trend of these figures using a five day moving average.

		Production in units	Trend in units
Week 1	Monday		
	Tuesday		
	Wednesday		
	Thursday		
	Friday		
Week 2	Monday		
	Tuesday		
	Wednesday		
	Thursday		
	Friday		
Week 3	Monday		
	Tuesday		
	Wednesday		
	Thursday		
	Friday		

(b) Calculate the average increase in the trend over the period.

(c)   The daily seasonal variations for this time series using the additive model have been calculated as follows:

Mon	Tue	Wed	Thu	Fri
−234.6	−13.8	+188	+177.8	−117.4

39

Using the trend and the seasonal variations, complete the table below to forecast the production volume for the following week.

Day	Trend in units	Seasonal variation	Forecast volume in units
Monday			
Tuesday			
Wednesday			
Thursday			
Friday			

(d) Each unit of production requires 0.5 hours of labour, which is paid at £8 per hour. All workers are paid weekly in arrears.

Use your answer in (c) to forecast the budgeted amount and timing of the cash payment for wages in Week 4.

3   It is December 20X8 and a business is preparing its cash budget for the first quarter of 20X9. The following sales and purchases figures have been produced:

	Sales in units	Purchases in units
January	5,000	5,200
February	5,600	5,800
March	5,700	5,500

The current cost of purchases is £20 per unit and these are sold for £35 per unit. The business has been informed by its supplier that purchase prices will be increased from 1 February 20X9 by 5% and the business has decided to increase its selling price by 8% from 1 January 20X9.

Purchases are all paid for in the month of purchase but the cash receipts from sales all occur in the month following the sale. Sales in December 20X8 were 4,800 units.

Use the table below to calculate the estimated cash inflows from sales and cash payments for purchases for January to March 20X9.

	Sales in units	Price per unit £	Cash inflow £	Purchases in units	Price per unit £	Cash outflow £
Jan						
Feb						
Mar						

4   A business has general overheads of £160,000 in September 20X9 but it is anticipated that these will increase by 1.75% per month for the next few months. Overheads are paid the month after they are incurred.

What is the cash outflow for overheads for the month of December 20X9?

	✓
£162,800	
£165,600	
£168,548	
£165,649	

5   A business makes purchases of a particular raw material which has a cost of £10.80 per kg in September 20X9. The actual and estimated specific price index for this material is as follows:

	Price index
September 20X9 (actual)	148.5
October 20X9 (estimate)	151.6
November 20X9 (estimate)	154.2
December 20X9 (estimate)	158.7

Complete the table below to calculate the expected price per kg (to the nearest penny) of the raw material in each of the months from October to December.

	Index calculation	Expected price £
October		
November		
December		

6   A business has budgeted the following purchases figures for the quarter:

October	£80,000
November	£97,000
December	£78,000

Each month it makes a mark-up on sales of 60%.

(a) Complete the table for the quarterly sales.

	Working	£
October sales		
November sales		
December sales		

Cash from sales is received 20% in the month of sale and 80% the month after.

(b) What is the cash received from customers in the month of December?

	✓
£124,800	
£130,880	
£149,120	
£155,200	

Patterns of cash flows

3

Learning outcomes

1.1	**Identify and classify different types of cash receipts and payments**
	Students need to be able to:
	• Identify the different types of cash receipts and cash payments, including regular, exceptional, capital, drawings, receipt of a loan from a bank, repayment of loan instalment and disbursements
2.1	**Prepare cash budgets and/or forecasts in the preferred format and clearly indicate net cash requirements, including the effects of lagged receipts and payments**
	Students need to be able to:
	• Evaluate the effect of lagged or delayed receipts and payments in the different periods of the cash budget, and the effect of settlement discounts, irrecoverable debts and timings

Assessment context

You need to be able to select a correct description from a list of options to match a type of cash receipt or cash payment.

You also need to be able to calculate sales receipts and cash payments for entry into a cash budget.

Qualification context

You will cover cash budgets again in the Level 4 paper *Management Accounting: Budgeting*.

Business context

Being able to establish predictable patterns in cash flows will improve the accuracy of forecasting.

Chapter overview

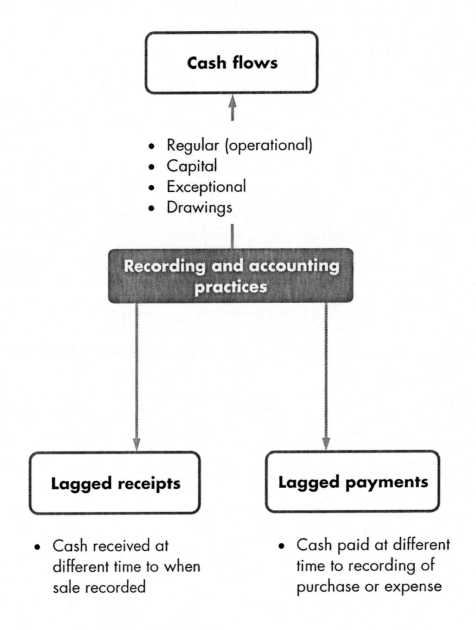

Cash flows

- Regular (operational)
- Capital
- Exceptional
- Drawings

Recording and accounting practices

Lagged receipts

- Cash received at different time to when sale recorded

Lagged payments

- Cash paid at different time to recording of purchase or expense

Introduction

In this chapter, we look at how to determine the cash flows that will impact the organisation. We consider the impact of credit on cash flows and other factors that result in timing differences. We also examine the forecasting of **exceptional items**.

1 Cash flows

Cash flows in and out of a business to maintain everyday operations. Cash also flows for other reasons.

Different types of business will incur different types of cash flows. The structure of the business will initially affect the type of cash flows. For example, a company may make regular annual dividend payments to its shareholders, whereas the amount and frequency of drawings that a sole trader takes out of the business will be their decision. A company will have to pay corporation tax on an annual basis, whereas a sole trader pays income tax out of personal income rather than out of the business.

The trade of the business will also affect the type of cash flows that the business has. For example, a supermarket will have a large amount of cash sales and purchases on credit but little or no sales on credit. In contrast, a manufacturing business may make all of its sales on credit with no immediate receipts of cash for goods sold.

Service industries will tend to have large, monthly expenses for wages and salaries but only a few payments for purchases, either on credit or for cash.

Activity 1: Types of cash flow

The different types of cash flow are listed below.

Required

Give an example of each type of cash flow.

Solution

		Receipts	Payments
(a)	Regular (Operational)		
(b)	Capital		
(c)	Exceptional		

1.1 Drawings

Drawings are amounts withdrawn from the organisation by its owners and can be either regular or irregular in nature.

1.2 Department cash flows

Consider the different types of information that different departments in a business would produce for a **cash budget** and how this information would be recorded. For example:

Department	Type of information	How is it recorded?
Sales	Expected cash and credit sales	Sales budget
Production	Expected levels of production and associated purchasing and other costs	Production and materials budget
Finance	Prices, costs, wages, overheads	Labour and expenses budgets
Treasury	Obtaining bank loans for short- and long-term finance. Plans for repayment of loan instalments	Finance budget
Senior management	Capital expenditure and sales, and plans for items such as the raising of additional capital or the payment of a dividend	Capital budget

1.3 Lagged receipts

If cash is received at a later time to when the sale was recorded, there is a **lagged receipt**. For example, a sale could be made on credit terms if payment is required 30 days after the invoice date. A business should know from experience the probable payment times for its customers. Unfortunately, sometimes a customer does not pay, and has no prospect of being able to. This debt is known as an **irrecoverable** debt and should be excluded from cash flow forecasts.

Illustration 1: Cash from customers

The fuel division of SC Fuel and Glass is preparing its quarterly cash flow forecast for each of the three months of October, November and December.

The sales of the fuel division for these three months are expected to be as follows:

October	£680,000
November	£700,000
December	£750,000

Of these sales, 20% are cash sales and the remainder are sales on credit. Experience has shown that, on average, the customers for credit sales pay the monies due with the following pattern:

The month after sale	20%
Two months after sale	50%
Three months after sale	30%

Therefore, the cash for the October credit sales will be received in November, December and January. If we are preparing the cash flow forecast for the period from October to December, then some of the cash inflows will be from credit sales in earlier periods. Therefore, you will also require information about the credit sales for these earlier periods.

The total sales in July to September for the fuel division (again 20% of these were cash sales) are:

July	£600,000
August	£560,000
September	£620,000

We can now start to piece together the information required to prepare the cash from sales for October to December:

Cash budget – October to December

	October £	November £	December £
Cash receipts:			
Cash sales (20% of month sales)	136,000	140,000	150,000

Now we need to deal with sales on credit which are more complicated and will require a working:

Working: Cash from credit sales

	October £	November £	December £
July sales (80% × 600,000 × 30%)	144,000		
August sales (80% × 560,000 × 50%)	224,000		
(80% × 560,000 × 30%)		134,400	
September sales (80% × 620,000 × 20%)	99,200		
(80% × 620,000 × 50%)		248,000	
(80% × 620,000 × 30%)			148,800
October sales (80% × 680,000 × 20%)		108,800	
(80% × 680,000 × 50%)			272,000
November sales (80% × 700,000 × 20%)			112,000
Cash from credit sales	467,200	491,200	532,800

Cash budget – October to December

	October £	November £	December £
Cash receipts: Cash sales	136,000	140,000	150,000
Cash from credit sales	467,200	491,200	532,800

Using the same information, we can also determine the closing trade receivables at the end of December, which is the cash from credit sales that has not yet been received:

		£
October sales	(80% × 680,000 × 30%)	163,200
November sales	(80% × 700,000 × 80%)	448,000
December sales	(80% × 750,000)	600,000
		1,211,200

Activity 2: Lagged receipts

Fred has just started in business and has forecast sales as follows:

January £125,000
February £150,000
March £175,000

All sales are on credit and 75% of each month's sales revenues will be received one month later.

The remaining revenue will be received two months after the sale.

Required

Forecast the cash receipts from January to March.

Solution

	January £	February £	March £
Cash received from invoices issued in:			
January			
February			
March			
Total receipts from sales			

A business may offer a **discount** to its customers if they pay their bills promptly. This discount will reduce the amount of the cash receipt. This is known as a **settlement discount**, and it is also referred to as '**discounts allowed**'.

Activity 3: Effect of discounts on receipts

George has forecast sales as follows: December £10,000; January £10,000; February £12,000; March £15,000.

Sales are partly for cash and partly on credit, as follows:

- 40% for cash (no discount)
- 60% on credit

A 5% discount is given to customers for payment within the current month and 25% of customers take up this option. All other cash is received in the month after the month of sale.

Required

What are the cash receipts for each of January to March?

Solution

	January £	February £	March £
Cash sales			
Credit sales			
Pay in same month			
Pay in next month			
Cash receipts			

1.4 Lagged payments

If cash is paid at a later time to the recording of the purchase or expense, it is a **lagged payment**.

Illustration 2: Payments to suppliers

The purchasing manager for SC Fuel and Glass has provided you with the following information about the anticipated purchases of fuel, for the fuel division, for the period October to December.

October	£408,000
November	£420,000
December	£450,000

The accounts department provides you with the following information about the payment pattern for these purchases, which are all made on credit terms:

- 25% of purchases are from suppliers who offer a 2% discount for payment in the month of the purchase and SC Fuel and Glass takes advantage of all such settlement discounts offered.

- 60% of purchases are paid in the month following the purchase.

- 15% are paid 2 months after the date of purchase.

This means that 25% of purchases are paid in the month of purchase with 2% deducted. The remaining 75% of purchases are paid for in the following 2 months. Therefore, we need information about the purchases in August and September in order to complete the cash flow forecast.

August purchases   £340,000
September purchases   £360,000

Again, we will need a working in order to determine the payments to suppliers in each of the three months.

Working: Payments to credit suppliers

	October £	November £	December £
August purchases (340,000 × 15%)	51,000		
September purchases (360,000 × 60%)	216,000		
(360,000 × 15%)		54,000	
October purchases (408,000 × 25% × 98%)	99,960		
(408,000 × 60%)		244,800	
(408,000 × 15%)			61,200
November purchases (420,000 × 25% × 98%)		102,900	
(420,000 × 60%)			252,000
December purchases (450,000 × 25% × 98%)			110,250
Payments to credit suppliers	366,960	401,700	423,450

Activity 4: Lagged payments

Arthur has produced the following purchasing estimates for the budgeted income statement:

January   £45,000
February   £65,000
March   £80,000

Purchases made in January must be paid for immediately. From then on, Arthur will get one month's credit from suppliers.

Required

How will the cash payments be forecast?

Solution

	January £	February £	March £
Payments for purchases			

2 Cash flow forecasting in practice

The basis of the cash flow forecast will be the budget prepared for the business plan or investment/divestment decision-making process.

Each line of income or expenditure can then be forecast in the appropriate manner, using the methodologies described above for unexceptional income and expenditure.

There may be a greater degree of uncertainty over some receipts and payments, and so a cash buffer may be kept to mitigate the impact of these. The general rule of prudence applies. The organisation may also have a policy of holding a buffer to deal with any unexpected items that may occur.

An unexpected item may be something such as chemical contamination on a building site which needs to be treated at additional cost before works can go ahead. Note that unexpected is not the same as exceptional.

The cash flow forecast is not a static document. It should be updated regularly, especially in light of any changes to the underlying assumptions or any significant unexpected items, and it can be refined as the impact of uncertain items becomes clearer. This is even more important with exceptional activities as, by their nature, they are less predictable than operations in the normal course of business.

Assessment focus point

1 All cash flows should be rounded to the nearest £.

2 In your assessment you may also be required to predict the value of the closing receivables and payables.

To do this, you will have to make certain assumptions, which could include some of the following:

- No change from prior year. If business conditions and volumes have stayed the same, this is a reasonable assumption to make.

- Increase or decrease by a certain percentage to allow for a change in business volume.

- Decrease by a certain percentage to allow for tighter credit management.

- Assume to be a certain percentage of the company's budgeted annual sales revenue for the year.

- Base the closing balances on the pattern of lagged receipts and payments used to predict the monthly cash flows.

Chapter summary

- When preparing a cash budget, one of the most complicated areas is normally cash receipts from sales.

- Receipts from cash sales will take place at the same time as the sale, but receipts from credit sales may be spread over a number of subsequent months. Any cash from credit sales still outstanding at the end of a particular period becomes the closing trade receivables balance.

- If irrecoverable debts are anticipated, then these are amounts that will not be received in cash and are therefore excluded from the cash budget.

- Payments for purchases on credit will also typically be spread over a number of future months. Any cash not yet paid to suppliers at the end of a particular period becomes the closing trade payables.

- If a settlement discount is offered on credit sales, then the amount of anticipated cash inflow must be reduced and if settlement discounts are taken on purchases, then the amount of the cash outflow must be reduced to reflect the smaller payment.

- Staff costs, overheads and capital purchases are examples of other types of expenditure that need to be accounted for in a cash budget.

- Exceptional items can be forecast according to the approved budget and plans that informed the original decision-making process.

Keywords

- **Cash budget:** A budget that shows the estimated cash inflows and outflows of the business for a specific period

- **Discounts allowed/Settlement discount:** Discount offered by the seller to the buyer in return for early payment of the amount due (also known as cash discount/prompt payment discount)

- **Exceptional item:** Income or payment that is unusual and not expected to recur

- **Irrecoverable debts:** Invoiced amounts that it is considered will never be received in cash

- **Lagged payment:** Payment of cash which takes place some time after the related transaction

- **Lagged receipt:** Receipt of cash which takes place some time after the related transaction

1 A business has estimates of the following sales figures:

	£
October	790,000
November	750,000
December	720,000
January	700,000
February	730,000
March	760,000

Of these total sales figures, 10% are likely to be cash sales and the remainder are credit sales. The payment pattern from customers in the past has been such that 40% of the total sales pay in the month after the sale and the remainder, 2 months after the month of sale. However, the business now expects that irrecoverable debts will amount to 5% of total sales, which will reduce the cash previously collected 2 months after sale.

Complete the table below to calculate the forecast cash receipts from sales for each of the months from January to March.

Forecast cash receipts

	Working	January £	February £	March £
Cash sales				
Credit sales				
Total receipts from sales				

2 A business has estimates of the following purchases figures:

	£
October	592,500
November	562,500
December	540,000
January	525,000
February	547,500
March	570,000

Purchases are all made on credit. 20% of purchases are offered a 2% discount for payment in the month after purchase and the business takes all such discounts. A further 65% of the purchases are paid for 2 months after the month of purchase and the remaining 15% are paid for 3 months after the date of purchase.

Complete the table below to calculate the cash payments for purchases for each of the months from January to March and the closing balance for trade payables at 31 March.

Forecast cash payments

	Working	January £	February £	March £	Closing trade payables £
October purchases					
November purchases					
December purchases					
January purchases					
February purchases					

	Working	January £	February £	March £	Closing trade payables £
March purchases					
Total payments for purchases/ trade payables at 31 March					

Preparing cash budgets 4

Learning outcomes

2.1	Prepare cash budgets and/or forecasts in the preferred format and clearly indicate net cash requirements, including the effects of lagged receipts and payments
	Students need to be able to:
	• Identify the range of information required that clearly identifies to the audience the net cash requirement
	• Prepare a cash budget format to include:
	– All sources of cash receipts totalled to show receipts for the period
	– All sources of cash payments totalled to show payments for the period
	– Net cash flow for the period
	– Opening cash balance
	– Closing cash balance
2.2	Undertake sensitivity analysis on cash budgets and make recommendations to management
	Students need to be able to:
	• Identify changes in assumptions, both controllable and non-controllable aspects, that can affect the cash budget
	• Calculate the impact of changes in volume, price, discounts and timings on the original cash budget
	• Make recommendations to management

Assessment context

You need to be able to calculate figures for inclusion in a cash budget. You will be required to enter figures into the correct parts of a cash budget layout.

Qualification context

You will also cover cash budgets in the Level 4 paper *Management Accounting: Budgeting*.

Business context

A cash budget shows the composition and timing of receipts and payments and changes in the net cash position. It therefore provides decision makers with an effective tool for cash management.

Chapter overview

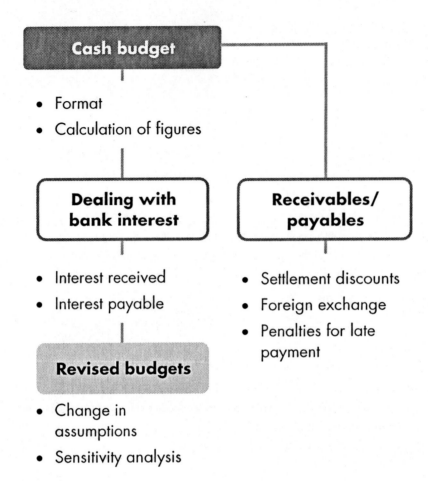

Cash budget

- Format
- Calculation of figures

Dealing with bank interest

- Interest received
- Interest payable

Revised budgets

- Change in assumptions
- Sensitivity analysis

Receivables/ payables

- Settlement discounts
- Foreign exchange
- Penalties for late payment

Introduction

This chapter will bring together much of the information studied in the previous chapters and consolidate it in the final preparation of the **cash budget**. Cash budgets provide decision makers with an effective tool for cash management which will be considered in the final chapters of this Course Book.

1 Cash budgets

Cash forecasting is vital to ensure that sufficient funds will be available when they are needed at an acceptable cost. Forecasts estimate:

- How much cash is required
- When it is required
- How long it is required for
- Whether it will be available from anticipated sources

A cash budget provides decision makers with an effective tool for cash management. They do not have a statutory format and can be presented in different ways.

For a cash budget to be useful, it should incorporate the following:

- Analysis of the sources of receipts leading to total receipts for the period
- Analysis of the sources of payments leading to total payments for the period
- Net cash flow for the period
- Bank balance brought forward
- Bank balance carried forward

The format of the cash budget aids decision making by showing the composition and timing of receipts and payments, and changes in the net cash position.

2 Approach to preparing a cash budget

A broad guideline to the preparation of a cash budget is shown below:

Step 1

Sort out cash receipts from customers:

- Establish budgeted sales month by month.

- Establish the credit period(s) taken by customers.

- Calculate when the budgeted sales revenue will be received as cash. Deduct any discount allowed for early payment.

- Establish when the outstanding receivables at the start of the budget period will pay.

Step 2

Establish whether any other cash income will be received, and when. Put these sundry items of cash receipts into the budget.

Step 3

Sort out cash payments to suppliers:

- Establish purchase quantities each month
- Establish the credit period(s) taken from suppliers
- Calculate when the cash payments to suppliers will be made
- Establish when the outstanding payables at the start of the budget period will be paid

Step 4

Establish other cash payments in the month.

These will include:

- Payments of wages and salaries
- Payments for sundry expenses
- Other one-off expenditures, such as non-current asset purchases and tax payments

Items of cost not involving cash payments (eg depreciation) must be excluded.

Payments should be scheduled into the month when they will actually occur.

Step 5

Set out the cash budget month by month. A commonly used general layout is:

Cash budget for the three months ending 31 March 20X5

	Jan £	Feb £	Mar £
Cash receipts:			
Receivables	X	X	X
Loan		X	
Total receipts	X	X	X
Cash payments:			
Payables	X	X	X
Wages	X	X	X
Overheads	X	X	X
Purchase of non-current assets	X		
Total payments	X	X	X

	Jan £	Feb £	Mar £
Net cash flow (receipts – payments)	X	(X)	X
Opening balance (b/f)	X	X	(X)
Closing balance (c/f)	X	(X)	X

Activity 1: St John's cash budget

St John's Ltd is a privately-owned college providing vocational training. The college provides part-time courses which are invoiced at the start of each academic term, and other courses which are invoiced throughout the year. The company has expanded in recent years and new classrooms are currently under construction at a cost of £300,000.

Today's date is 5 January 20X2. The following information has been provided:

- The balance on the cash account at the end of December 20X1 was £13,230.

- Receivables:

	Invoiced sales £	Outstanding receivables at 31.12.20X1 £
September	184,000	25,250
October	20,000	3,250
November	11,000	2,980

All outstanding amounts from customers at 31 December 20X1 will be received by 31 January 20X2. No sales invoices were issued in December.

- There will be 184 students who will each be billed £1,250 in January for their studies for the three months to 31 March 20X2.

- £20,000 will be billed for other courses in February and £30,000 in March.

- The budgeted cash inflow from sales invoices will be:

  50% in the month the invoice is issued

  30% one month after the invoice is issued

  20% two months after the invoice is issued

- From 1 February, the college will start selling stationery to students in the college shop. Sales will be for cash and are expected to total £400 each month with a cost of sales of £280.

- Monthly staff salaries and administration costs should be increased from 1 January to include an inflation allowance of 3% above the actual costs for December. The salary cost in December was £35,000 and administration costs were £17,200. These costs will then remain constant for both February and March.

- Repairs and maintenance expenditure will be £6,000 in January and February, and £10,000 in March.

- College supplies will amount to £16,500 each month. College supplies will be paid for one month in arrears. At 31 December 20X1, the amount owed for college supplies was £6,300.

- Salaries, repairs and maintenance, stationery for the shop and administration costs will be paid for in the month in which they are incurred.

- The remaining £240,000 for construction costs is due to be paid on 31 March 20X2.

Required

Prepare a cash budget for each of the three months ending 31 March 20X2.

Solution

Workings

	January £	February £	March £
Cash receipts:			
From opening receivables (W1)			
January invoices (W2)			
February invoices (W3)			
March invoices (W4)			
Shop sales			
Total receipts			
Cash payments:			
Salaries (W5)			
Repairs and maintenance			
College supplies			
Administration costs (W6)			
Costs of stationery sales			
Capital expenditure			

	January £	February £	March £
Total payments			
Net cash flow (receipts – payments)			
Opening balance (b/f)			
Closing balance (c/f)			

 Assessment focus point

In the assessment you will be expected to produce a cash budget for at least two periods and all cash budget figures should be rounded to whole pounds, following normal conventions.

2.1 Dealing with bank interest

Bank interest may need to be incorporated into a cash budget:

* Interest received from positive cash balances
* Interest payable on a bank overdraft

Check the interest rate carefully. If an annual rate is quoted, you need to divide this rate by 12 months for a monthly rate.

Illustration 1: Finance charges

Assume a cash budget to date appears as follows:

Cash budget – October to December

	October £	November £	December £
Cash receipts:			
Cash sales	136,000	140,000	150,000
Cash from credit sales	467,200	491,200	532,800
Sale of non-current asset		9,000	9,000
Total cash receipts	603,200	640,200	691,800
Cash payments:			
Payments for credit purchases	366,960	401,700	423,450
Wages and salaries	113,000	113,000	113,000
General overheads	68,000	73,250	75,000
Capital expenditure			120,000
Sales tax (VAT)	45,000		
Total cash payments	592,960	587,950	731,450
Net cash flow for the month	10,240	52,250	(39,650)
Opening cash balance	(29,500)	(19,260)	32,990
Closing cash balance	(19,260)	32,990	(6,660)

At the end of September, there is an overdraft balance of £29,500 and at the end of October, an overdraft balance of £19,260. Say that interest is incurred at 1% per month on these balances and charged in the following month. Therefore, a further cash outflow line must be included for overdraft interest, based upon the balance at the end of the previous month. This, in turn, will have an effect on the net cash flow for the month and the overdraft balance at the end of October.

The overdraft interest cash payment in October will be based upon the overdraft balance at 30 September:

$$1\% \times £29,500 = £295$$

This is entered as a cash outflow which, in turn, means that the overdraft balance at the end of October will increase to £19,555. Therefore, the overdraft interest in November will be:

$$1\% \times £19,555 = £196$$

Cash budget – October to December

	October £	November £	December £
Cash receipts:			
Cash sales	136,000	140,000	150,000
Cash from credit sales	467,200	491,200	532,800
Sale of non-current assets		9,000	9,000
Total cash receipts	603,200	640,200	691,800
Cash payments:			
Payments for credit purchases	366,960	401,700	423,450
Wages and salaries	113,000	113,000	113,000
General overheads	68,000	73,250	75,000
Capital expenditure			120,000
Sales tax (VAT)	45,000		
Overdraft interest	295	196	
Total cash payments	593,255	588,146	731,450
Net cash flow for the month	9,945	52,054	(39,650)
Opening cash balance	(29,500)	(19,555)	32,499
Closing cash balance	(19,555)	32,499	(7,151)

Note that the introduction of the overdraft interest has affected each of the month-end balances.

If you are told that interest is receivable on credit balances, then the procedure is the same as for overdraft interest but is a cash inflow:

- Calculate the interest based upon the balance at the end of the previous period.
- Include as a cash inflow in the following month.

Activity 2: Bank interest in cash budget

The following cash budget figures have been calculated before taking account of bank interest.

	January £	February £	March £
Total receipts	13,000	15,500	16,100
Total payments	21,600	19,500	17,600

The bank pays interest at 0.2% per month on the closing credit balance of the previous month. It charges interest of 0.75% per month on overdrawn balances.

The bank balance at the end of December was £11,000.

Required

Calculate the forecast closing cash balance in March.

Solution

	January £	February £	March £
Receipts before interest			
Interest received @ 0.2%			
Total receipts			
Payments before interest			
Interest paid @ 0.75%			
Total payments			
Net cash flow (receipts – payments)			
Opening balance (b/f)			
Closing balance (c/f)			

3 Settlement discounts

Whether or not to offer or accept a settlement discount is a decision that needs to be assessed. An early settlement discount involves setting a lower price in exchange for the customer paying early. Typically, this is shown as a percentage of the invoiced value, so for example, a 2% discount for payment two weeks before the invoice due date.

The financial consideration is whether or not getting the money early is worth the 2% of income that has been forgone; however, this is not the only point to think about.

3.1 Offering early settlement discounts

There are several reasons that a business may offer a settlement discount to its customers:

- Improve liquidity by reducing the working capital cycle. If the business is suffering from cash flow problems, then this will be especially important.

- The cost of other short-term finance, such as overdraft interest, will be reduced if the other sources of finance are more expensive than the cost of the discount.

- If customers prioritise payment of the discounted invoices in order to take advantage of the reduced cost, then the likelihood of bad debts is reduced.

- It can improve the competitiveness of the business, as it is essentially offering a discount on the price of the products.

There are also downsides to offering early settlement discount:

- As the last point implies, settlement discounts are essentially a reduction in the prices of the products, and so the business should consider the financial implications of offering these.

- Administratively, it can be difficult to recover deductions from customers who have paid too late to qualify for the discount, but have still applied it to their payment.

A company should weigh up the pros and cons of offering discounts carefully before going ahead with them.

You should also be aware that if an early settlement discount is offered, the VAT is calculated on the sales amount net of the settlement discount, and this is applicable, even if the early settlement discount is not taken up.

Illustration 2: Early settlement discounts

SC Fuel and Glass has an overdraft on its current account of £500,000. The simple annual interest rate charged on this overdraft is 20% with interest applied annually.

In order to reduce its overdraft, the company is considering offering early settlement discounts to customers who pay within 7 days, rather than the normal terms of 45 days.

It is possible to quantify the maximum discount that the business should offer:

The business is effectively paying (by sacrificing some of the sales value) to receive its cash (45 – 7) 38 days early. Therefore, the maximum discount should be the effective interest rate that the business is paying on its overdraft for the 38 days.

To calculate the interest rate:

$$20\% \div 365 = 0.0548\% \text{ per day}$$

For 38 days this is equivalent to:

$$0.0548 \times 38 = 2.0824\%$$

So, the maximum discount that should be offered to customers to encourage them to pay early is 2.0824%.

This assumes a simple rate of interest, because interest on the overdraft was being applied annually.

If the interest rate is a **compound interest rate** with the interest being applied daily, then the maximum discount can be found using the formula:

$$\left((1+r)^{d/365} - 1 \right) \times 100$$

Where   r = annual rate

d = number of days that the cash receipt is accelerated

Using the same information as above, but for an account with compound daily interest, the interest saved on the overdraft would be:

$$= \left((1.2)^{38/365} - 1 \right) \times 100$$

$$= 1.916\%$$

So, the maximum discount that should be offered is 1.916%.

4 Revised budgets

Cash budgets are prepared using **assumptions** about the nature of cash flows. Net cash requirements will be affected by changes in those assumptions and revised cash budgets will need to be prepared.

If the cash budget is prepared on a well-designed spreadsheet, it is easy to revise the budget or perform 'what if' calculations. This is also called **sensitivity analysis**. For example, what if sales are 10% lower than expected? What if the timing of cash receipts from receivables changes?

Activity 3: St John's cash budget – revised

Using the information in St John's cash budget, revise the cash budget to show the impact of a 20% increase in students enrolling in January; and inflation of 4% instead of 3%.

Some of the information that remains unchanged has already been re-entered in the cash budget below.

Required

Revise and complete the cash budget in the light of the new information mentioned above.

Solution

	January £	February £	March £
Cash receipts:			
From opening receivables	31,480		
January invoices			
February invoices		10,000	6,000
March invoices			15,000
Shop sales		400	400
Total receipts			
Cash payments:			
Salaries			
Repairs and maintenance	6,000	6,000	10,000
College supplies	6,300	16,500	16,500
Administration costs			
Costs of stationery sales		280	280
Capital expenditure			240,000
Total payments			
Net cash flow (receipts – payments)			
Opening balance (b/f)	13,230		
Closing balance (c/f)			

4.1 Receipts or payments in a foreign currency

Cash budgets may involve receipts or payments in a foreign currency.

4.1.1 Receipts in a foreign currency

Where a receipt in a foreign currency is expected in the next few months, there is a risk of the exchange rate moving in such a way that fewer pounds are received. This is sometimes referred to as transaction risk.

The risk is that over this period, the pound gets **stronger** – UK exporters suffer because the overseas currency eg the dollar is getting weaker and their revenues are in dollars.

For example, if a UK exporter sells items to an American customer for $1,000 when the exchange rate is $2:£1, the UK exporter would be expecting $1,000/2 = £500 revenue today. However, if the sale was on three months' credit, and in three months' time the pound was expected to strengthen by, for example, 25% to $2.50:£1, then the sterling receipt would be $1,000/2.5 = £400. Strengthening by 25% means it costs 25% more dollars to buy £1, so $2 × 125% = $2.50:£1.

Activity 4: Drax

Drax plc is a UK manufacturer of air-conditioning systems and does a significant amount of business in mainland Europe. The company has just delivered a major export order to a customer in Luxembourg at a price of €35 million, payable in six months' time.

As the company's assistant accountant, you are concerned about the potential impact of currency volatility on the profitability of this major order.

Today's exchange rate (the spot rate) is 1.376 euros per pound.

The euro/pound exchange rate has been volatile in recent months, and there is a significant chance that the value of the pound may increase or decrease by up to 5% over the next six months.

Required

(a) **Calculate the expected revenue in £s from this order if the exchange rate in six months' time is unchanged (work to the nearest £):**

(b) **Calculate the increase or (decrease) in revenue in £s that will result from a 5% increase in the value of the pound (work to the nearest £):**

(c) **Calculate the increase or (decrease) in revenue in £s that will result from a 5% decrease in the value of the pound (work to the nearest £):**

(d) **Advise which movement in the exchange rate is harmful for Drax.**

Select one:

Decrease in the value of the pound

Increase in the value of the pound

4.1.2 Payments in a foreign currency

Where a payment in a foreign currency is due in the next few months, there is a risk of the exchange rate moving in such a way that the invoice costs more in the local currency (eg pounds). This is another example of transaction risk.

The risk is that over this period, the pound gets **weaker** – UK importers suffer because the overseas currency eg the dollar is getting stronger and their costs are denominated in dollars.

Note. Exchange rates may be given per pound or per unit of the foreign currency. In the previous example (Drax) the exchange rate of 1.376 euros per pound could have been given as 0.72674 pounds **per euro**. If you prefer to deal with exchange rates as **euros per pound** you can convert the exchange rate of 0.72674 pounds per euro into euros per pound eg 1/0.72674 = 1.376.

4.2 Penalties for late payment

Another issue that you may come across as you create a cash budget is that suppliers may charge a fee for late payment.

For example, if a company is due to pay a supplier £100,000 one month in arrears, but intends to pay after two months (ie one month late), then the company will need to budget for any penalty imposed by the supplier. If the supplier charges interest of 3% per year on late payments, then the penalty for paying one month late will be:

3% per year/12 months = 0.25% per month

£100,000 × 0.0025 = £250

Chapter summary

- In order to prepare a cash budget, information will be required from many different sources within the organisation.

- Care must be taken with the timing of other cash flows, such as overheads, which may not necessarily all be paid in the month incurred – any non-cash flows such as depreciation charges must be excluded from the cash flow forecast.

- If information is given about overdraft interest, then this must be calculated each month, based upon the overdraft balance at the start of the month and shown as a cash outflow.

- If information is given about bank interest receivable on credit balances, then this must be calculated, based upon the balance at the start of the month and shown as a cash inflow.

- If there are changes in estimates or assumptions used in the cash budget, then these must be put through with an altered cash budget in subsequent periods.

- Settlement discounts are essentially a reduction in the prices of products, and so a business should quantify the financial implications of offering these to customers. The cost of the discount can be compared to the overdraft interest saved by receiving cash from the customer earlier.

- A cash budget may be prepared using certain assumptions about the level of irrecoverable debts or the available prompt payment discounts. If these assumptions change, then the cash flows to be incorporated in the budget will need to be revised accordingly (sensitivity analysis).

Keywords

- **Cash budget:** A budget that shows the estimated cash inflows and outflows of the business for a specific period

- **Sensitivity analysis:** A technique that can be used to assess the impact that changing a particular assumption will have on the budget

1 A business is about to prepare a cash budget for the quarter ending 31 December. The estimated sales figures are as follows:

	£
September (estimate)	360,000
October (estimate)	400,000
November (estimate)	450,000
December (estimate)	460,000

All sales are on credit and the payment pattern is as follows:

20% pay in the month of sale, after taking a 5% settlement discount.

80% pay in the month following the sale.

(a) Complete the table below in order to calculate the receipts from credit sales for the quarter ending 31 December.

	October £	November £	December £

The purchases of the business are all on credit and it is estimated that the following purchases will be made:

	£
August	200,000
September	220,000
October	240,000
November	270,000
December	280,000

30% of purchases are paid for in the month after the purchase has been made and the remainder are paid for two months after the month of purchase.

(b) Complete the table below to calculate the payments for purchases on credit for the three months ending 31 December.

	October £	November £	December £

General overheads are anticipated to be £30,000 for each of September and October, increasing to £36,000 thereafter. 80% of the general overheads are paid for in the month in which they are incurred and the remainder, in the following month. Included in the general overheads figure is a depreciation charge of £5,000 each month.

(c) Complete the table below to calculate the cash payments for general overheads for each month for the three months ending 31 December.

	October £	November £	December £

Additional information

- Gross wages are expected to be £42,000 each month and are paid in the month in which they are incurred.

- Selling expenses are anticipated to be 5% of the monthly sales value and are paid for in the month following the sale.

- The business has planned to purchase new equipment for £40,000 in November and in the same month, to dispose of old equipment, with estimated sales proceeds of £4,000.

- If the business has an overdraft balance at the start of the month, then there is an interest charge that month of 1% of the overdraft balance. At 1 October, it is anticipated that the business will have an overdraft of £50,000.

(d) **Referring to your answers in parts (a), (b) and (c) and the additional information above, prepare a monthly cash budget for the three months ending 31 December. Cash inflows should be entered as positive figures and cash outflows as negative figures.**

Cash budget for the quarter ending 31 December

	October £	November £	December £
Cash receipts:			
Sales proceeds from equipment			
Receipts from sales			
Total receipts			
Cash payments:			
Payments for purchases			
Wages			
General overheads			
Selling expenses			
New equipment			
Overdraft interest			
Total payments			
Net cash flow			
Opening balance			
Closing balance			

2 A manufacturing business is to prepare its cash budget for the three months commencing 1 October. The business manufactures a product called the gleep, which requires two hours of labour per completed gleep. The labour force is paid at a rate of £7.50 per hour. Each gleep sells for £60.

The forecast sales of gleeps are as follows:

Forecast sales – units of gleeps

August	September	October	November	December
7,000	7,200	6,800	7,400	7,500

Sales are on credit, with 60% of customers paying in the month after sale and the remainder, two months after the sale.

The production for gleeps is as follows (units):

September	October	November	December
7,200	6,700	7,300	7,400

(a) Complete the table below to calculate the cash receipts from sales for the three months ending December.

	October £	November £	December £
Total receipts from sales			

The raw materials required for production are purchased in the month prior to production and 40% are paid for in the following month and the remainder, two months after purchase. Material usage figures are as follows:

	£
September	172,800
October	163,200
November	178,800
December	175,200

(b) **Complete the table below to calculate the amount paid for purchases in each of the three months from October to December.**

	October £	November £	December £
Total payments for purchases			

Additional information

- The production staff gross wages are paid in the month in which they are incurred.

- Production overheads are anticipated to be 40% of the materials used in each month and are paid for in the month in which they are incurred.

- General overheads are anticipated to be £64,000 in each of October and November, increasing to £70,000 in December, and are paid in the month in which they are incurred. The figure for general overheads includes £12,000 of depreciation each month.

- The cash balance at 1 October is expected to be £20,000 in hand.

(c) **Referring to your answers to parts (a) and (b) and the additional information above, prepare a monthly cash budget for the three months ending December. Cash inflows should be entered as positive figures; and cash outflows, as figures in brackets.**

	October £	November £	December £
Cash receipts:			
Sales			
Cash payments:			
Purchases			
Wages			
Production overheads			
General overheads			

	October £	November £	December £
Total payments			
Net cash flow			
Opening balance			
Closing balance			

3   A company is organising its annual staff meeting. It has checked prices and found that the following early payment discounts apply.

	Advance cost £	Advance payment Days	On the day cost £
Train fares	180.00	14	750.00
Hotel room	9,500.00	60	9,600.00
Dinner	150.00	28	170.00

The company's cost of finance is 15% per annum, charged on a simple annual interest rate.

Which of the discounts should the company accept?

	Discount %	Cost of finance %	Accept?
Train fares			
Hotel room			
Dinner			

Monitoring cash flows

5

Learning outcomes

2.3	Identify deviations from the cash budget and recommend corrective action within organisational policies
	Students need to be able to:
	• Identify and explain deviations from the cash budget and given information with possible courses of action to address the deviation from the cash budget and controls to prevent further recurrence
	• Explain the importance of preparing a cash budget, evaluating the strengths and weaknesses of cash budgets as a monitoring tool for organisations

Assessment context

You need to be able to calculate deviations from a budget and identify actions that could be taken to deal with variances.

Qualification context

You will cover variance analysis for sales and costs in the Level 4 papers *Management Accounting: Decision and Control* and *Management Accounting: Budgeting*.

Business context

Cash management is not just about being able to prepare a cash budget. It also involves being able to identify and quantify deviations from budget so that action can be taken.

Chapter overview

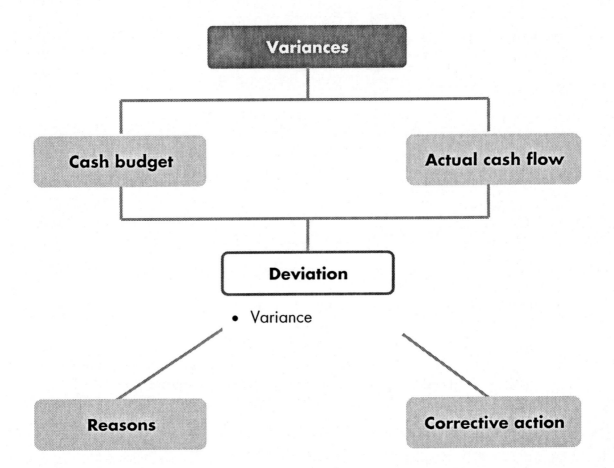

- Variance

Introduction

We have seen how a cash budget can be used to predict cash shortfalls and cash surpluses. A cash budget can also be used to **monitor and control** cash inflows and outflows.

1 Cash flow variances

If there are **significant differences** between the actual and expected cash flows, then management can investigate the reasons for these differences and take action to ensure that cash flows and balances revert to plan.

Actual cash flows can be compared with forecast cash flows to calculate **deviations** or **variances**. This process is known as **variance analysis**.

Illustration 1: Cash flow variances (1)

Given below is the cash budget for the fuel division of SC for the month of June, together with the actual cash flows for the month.

Cash budget: June

	Budgeted cash flows £	Actual cash flows £
Receipts:		
Cash sales	110,000	106,500
Receipts from credit customers	655,000	633,000
Proceeds from sale of non-current assets	–	15,000
Total receipts	765,000	754,500
Payments:		
Payments to credit suppliers	550,000	589,000
Wages	108,000	108,000
Rent	10,000	10,500
Advertising	12,000	9,000
Purchase of non-current assets	–	27,000
Dividend payment	20,000	20,000
Total payments	700,000	763,500
Net cash flow	65,000	(9,000)
Opening cash balance	10,000	10,000
Closing cash balance	75,000	1,000

Note how the actual net cash flow is a cash outflow, shown in brackets, as the total payments in the month were greater than the total receipts.

We can now compare the actual and budgeted figures for each line of the cash budget to discover the differences or variances.

	Budgeted cash flows £	Actual cash flows £	Variance £
Cash sales:	110,000	106,500	(3,500)
Receipts from credit customers	655,000	633,000	(22,000)
Proceeds from sale of non-current assets	–	15,000	15,000
Total receipts	765,000	754,500	
Payments:			
Payments to credit suppliers	550,000	589,000	(39,000)
Wages	108,000	108,000	–
Rent	10,000	10,500	(500)
Advertising	12,000	9,000	3,000
Purchase of non-current assets	–	27,000	(27,000)
Dividend payment	20,000	20,000	–
Total payments	700,000	763,500	
Net cash flow	65,000	(9,000)	(74,000)
Opening cash balance	10,000	10,000	–
Closing cash balance	75,000	1,000	(74,000)

Any difference which is good news, such as receipts being higher than budgeted, or payments being lower than budgeted, are known as **favourable variances**.

Any differences which are bad news, where receipts are less than budgeted or payments are greater than budgeted, are known as **adverse variances**. The adverse variances are shown in brackets.

Activity 1: Cash flow variances

St John's Ltd is a privately owned college providing vocational training. The college provides part-time courses which are invoiced at the start of each academic term, and other courses which are invoiced throughout the year. The company has expanded in recent years and new classrooms are currently under construction at a cost of £300,000.

The **actual** cash flows for each of the three months ended 31 December 20X4 were as follows:

	October £	November £	December £
Cash received from invoices issued in:			
September	54,100	11,150	1,500
October	8,450	3,100	5,200
November	0	5,400	2,620
Salaries	(35,000)	(35,000)	(35,000)
Repairs and maintenance	(5,400)	(5,210)	(4,800)
College supplies	(15,480)	(16,300)	(8,150)
Administration costs	(16,930)	(17,220)	(17,200)
Dividend	(50,000)	0	0
Capital expenditure	0	0	(60,000)
Movement for 3-month period	(60,260)	(54,080)	(115,830)
Cash b/f	243,400	183,140	129,060
Cash c/f	183,140	129,060	13,230

The **budgeted** cash flow for the three months to 31 December 20X4:

	October £	November £	December £
Cash received from invoices issued in:			
September	55,200	36,800	0
October	15,000	9,000	6,000
November	0	6,000	3,600
Salaries	(35,000)	(35,000)	(35,000)
Repairs and maintenance	(1,400)	(2,400)	(2,400)
College supplies	(15,000)	(16,000)	(8,000)
Administration costs	(17,000)	(17,000)	(17,000)
Capital expenditure	0	0	(60,000)
Movement for month	1,800	(18,600)	(112,800)

	October £	November £	December £
Cash b/f	243,400	245,200	226,600
Cash c/f	245,200	226,600	113,800

Required

Compare the actual cash flows with forecast cash flows and calculate deviations.

Solution

	Actual cash 3-month total £	Forecast cash 3-month total £	Variance £
Cash received from invoices issued in:			
September			
October			
November			
Salaries			
Repairs and maintenance			
College supplies			
Administration costs			
Dividend			
Capital expenditure			
Movement for month			
Cash b/f			
Cash c/f			

Deviations from the cash budget can be summarised by **reconciling** budgeted cash flow with actual cash flow.

Illustration 2: Cash flow variances (2)

Again we will use the cash flow forecast and actual figures for June for the fuel division of SC.

	June	
	Budgeted cash flows £	Actual cash flows £
Receipts:		
Cash sales	110,000	106,500
Receipts from credit customers	655,000	633,000
Proceeds from sale of non-current assets	–	15,000
Total receipts	765,000	754,500
Payments:		
Payments to credit suppliers	550,000	589,000
Wages	108,000	108,000
Rent	10,000	10,500
Advertising	12,000	9,000
Purchase of non-current assets	(11)	27,000
Dividend payment	20,000	20,000
Total payments	700,000	763,500
Net cash flow	65,000	(9,000)
Opening cash balance	10,000	10,000
Closing cash balance	75,000	1,000

Again, the variance for each line of the cash flow forecast is calculated:

	June		
	Budgeted cash flows £	Actual cash flows £	Variance £
Receipts:			
Cash sales	110,000	106,500	(3,500)
Receipts from credit customers	655,000	633,000	(22,000)
Proceeds from sale of non-current assets	–	15,000	15,000
Total receipts	765,000	754,500	
Payments:			
Payments to credit suppliers	550,000	589,000	(39,000)
Wages	108,000	108,000	–
Rent	10,000	10,500	(500)
Advertising	12,000	9,000	3,000
Purchase of non-current assets	–	27,000	(27,000)
Dividend payment	20,000	20,000	–
Total payments	700,000	763,500	
Net cash flow	65,000	(9,000)	(74,000)
Opening cash balance	10,000	10,000	–
Closing cash balance	75,000	1,000	(74,000)

These figures are then used to explain why the actual cash balance at the end of June was £1,000 when it had been budgeted to be £75,000.

This is normally done by starting with the budgeted cash balance and adding any favourable variances and deducting any adverse variances.

June – reconciliation of actual cash balance to budgeted cash balance

	£
Budgeted cash balance	75,000
Shortfall in cash sales	(3,500)
Shortfall in receipts from customers	(22,000)
Additional receipt from sale of non-current asset	15,000
Additional payments to credit suppliers	(39,000)
Additional rent	(500)
Lower advertising cost	3,000
Additional non-current asset purchase	(27,000)
Actual cash balance	1,000

Activity 2: Reconciling cash flows

Required

Summarise the deviations from cash budget in the cash flow variances activity above by reconciling budgeted cash flow with actual cash flow. Use the picklists to select the correct word in each line in the reconciliation.

Solution

	£
Budgeted cash balance at 31 December 20X4	
(Excess/Shortfall) in invoice receipts	
(Increase/Decrease) in repairs and maintenance expenditure	
(Increase/Decrease) in college supplies	
(Increase/Decrease) in administration expenditure	
(Budgeted/Unbudgeted) dividend	
Actual cash balance at 31 December 20X4	

2 Reasons for differences

Once variances have been identified, possible reasons for these differences need to be identified.

- Has there been a change in underlying volumes?
- Have prices changed?
- Has the timing of receipts or payments changed?

Assessment focus point

The table below is not an exhaustive list of the causes of variances, and an assessment question might suggest other possible causes. You should review the information provided and select any causes that are consistent with the reported variances.

Variance	Favourable	Adverse
(a) Material price	Unforeseen discounts received More care taken in purchasing Change in quality of material	Price increase Careless purchasing Change in quality of material
(b) Material usage	Material used of higher quality More effective use made of material Errors in allocating material to jobs	Defective material Excessive waste Theft Stricter quality control Errors in allocating material to jobs
(c) Labour rate	Use of workers at a rate of pay lower than standard	Wage rate increase Use of higher grade labour
(d) Labour efficiency	Output produced more quickly than expected because of work motivation, better quality of equipment or materials, or better methods Errors in allocating time to jobs	Lost time in excess of time allowed Output lower than expected because of deliberate restriction, lack of training, or sub-standard material used Errors in allocating time to jobs

If the variances are significant, **corrective action** should be taken.

Recommended action must consider the impact on the cash position of the organisation and on organisational policies.

Activity 3: Causes of variances

Required

Suggest possible actions for the causes of variances listed in the table.

Solution

Cause of variance	Possible actions
Delayed receipts from credit sales	
Reduced sales volumes	
Increased volume of purchases	
Increased purchase prices	
Payments made too soon	
Increased labour costs	

Activity 4: Significant deviations and control action

Required

Using the information from the cash flow variances activity above, identify three significant deviations from the cash budget and suggest what action could have been taken to avoid each of these variances.

Solution

(1)

(2)

(3)

BPP
LEARNING MEDIA

Chapter summary

- Cash budgets show the expected receipts and payments during a budget period and are a vital management planning and control tool.

- As part of the management role of control, it is important to compare the actual cash flows for a period to the budgeted or forecast cash flows – this can be done by calculating variances on a line by line basis or by reconciling the actual cash balance to the budgeted cash balance.

- Variances measure the difference between actual results and expected results. The process by which the total difference between standard and actual results is analysed is known as variance analysis.

- Once the variances between actual and budgeted cash flows have been determined, they may be investigated and appropriate actions taken.

- There are a wide range of reasons for the occurrence of adverse and favourable cost variances.

- A cash budget, once prepared, can indicate to management future cash surpluses or deficits and can also indicate areas where procedures and policies can be altered or improved in order to improve the cash position.

Keywords

- **Adverse variances:** Variances which represent less income or greater expense than budgeted

- **Control:** An essential element of management in an organisation to ensure that plans are met

- **Favourable variances:** Variances which represent greater income or less expense than budgeted

- **Variances:** The difference between actual results and budgeted results

Test your learning

1   Given below is the cash budget for Glenn Security Systems for the month of May, together with the actual cash flows for the month.

    (a) Identify and quantify three significant differences/variances between the actual cash flow for the month and the budgeted cash flow.

        •

        •

        •

    (b) Suggest three actions that the company could have taken to avoid using its overdraft facility.

        •

        •

        •

Cash budget: May

	Budget £	Actual £
Cash sales receipts	43,000	45,000
Credit sales receipts	256,000	231,000
Credit suppliers	(176,000)	(189,000)
Wages	(88,000)	(88,000)
Overheads	(43,200)	(44,500)
Capital expenditure	–	(40,000)
Movement for the month	(8,200)	(85,500)
Bank b/f	53,400	52,100
Bank c/f	45,200	(33,400)

2 Given below is the cash budget for Glenn Security Systems for the month of May, together with the actual cash flows for the month.

	Budget £	Actual £
Cash sales receipts	43,000	45,000
Credit sales receipts	256,000	231,000
Payments to credit suppliers	(176,000)	(189,000)
Wages	(88,000)	(88,000)
Overheads	(43,200)	(44,500)
Capital expenditure	–	(40,000)
Movement for the month	(8,200)	(85,500)
Bank b/f	53,400	52,100
Bank c/f	45,200	(33,400)

Prepare a reconciliation of the budgeted closing cash balance with the actual closing cash balance for the month.

	£
Budgeted cash balance at 31 May	
Surplus/shortfall in receipts from cash sales	
Surplus/shortfall in receipts from credit sales	
Surplus/shortfall in payments to credit suppliers	
Increase/decrease in overheads	
Increase/decrease in capital expenditure	
Lower opening cash balance	
Actual cash balance at 31 May	

3　Given below are the cash budgets for the quarter ending 30 June for Davies Engineering. The company has an agreed overdraft facility of £20,000.

Cash budget

	April £	May £	June £
Receipts:			
Cash sales	64,000	75,000	78,000
Receipts from credit customers	489,000	470,000	449,000
Proceeds from sale of non-current assets	–	10,000	–
Total receipts	553,000	555,000	527,000
Payments:			
Payments to credit suppliers	426,000	437,000	425,000
Wages	84,000	84,000	84,000
Rent	8,000	8,000	8,000
Capital expenditure	26,000	28,000	–
Sales tax (VAT)	–	12,200	
Training costs	20,000		
Repairs and maintenance	10,400		
Total payments	574,400	569,200	517,000
Net cash flow	(21,400)	(14,200)	10,000
Opening cash balance	2,600	(18,800)	(33,000)
Closing cash balance	(18,800)	(33,000)	(23,000)

Which of the following courses of action could improve the cash forecast position and keep the company within its agreed overdraft limit?

(i)　Improve credit collection and speed up receipts from credit customers
(ii)　Sell non-current asset earlier or arrange for cash to be received earlier
(iii)　Increase credit period taken from suppliers by paying later
(iv)　Delay capital expenditure in April and May
(v)　Finance capital expenditure differently eg bank loan
(vi)　Delay training courses
(vii)　Negotiate credit terms for repairs and maintenance costs

	✓
(i), (iii), (iv), (vii)	
(i), (ii), (v), (vi), (vii)	
(i), (ii), (v), (vii)	
(i), (iii), (iv), (v), (vi), (vii)	

4   A company prepares annual budgets for its profits, including detailed budgets for sales, materials and labour. Departmental managers are allowed to revise their budgets if they believe there have been planning errors.

The managing director has become concerned that recent budget revisions have meant that there are favourable variances but less profit than expected.

Two specific situations have recently arisen, for which budget revisions were sought:

Components

A supplier of an essential component was forced into liquidation. The company managed to find another supplier overseas at short notice. This second supplier charged more for the components and also added a delivery charge. The component was needed urgently and so the price was agreed. Two months later another, more competitive, local supplier was found and is now being used.

A budget revision is being sought for the two months where higher prices had to be paid.

Labour

During the early part of the year, the company experienced problems with the quality of work being produced. The departmental manager had complained that his team were complacent and had not attempted to keep up with new developments in the industry.

The company therefore changed its policy so as to recruit staff with excellent reputations for innovation on short-term contracts. This has had the effect of pushing up the costs involved but increasing productivity.

The departmental manager has requested a budget revision to cover the extra costs involved, following the change of policy.

Discuss each request for a budget revision, putting what you see as both sides of the argument and conclude whether a budget revision should be allowed.

Liquidity management

6

Learning outcomes

3.2	**Discuss the principles of liquidity management** Students need to know: • The importance of cash budgeting to liquidity management • The importance of ensuring that an organisation can make its financial commitments on time • The working capital cycle and the cash cycle • How to recognise liquid and non-liquid assets • Return on capital employed and current ratio • Liquidity ratios and their importance in liquidity management • The effect on cash flow in respect of the timing of payments received and payments made in determining the cash budget • Signs of overtrading and overcapitalisation
3.3	**Discuss how an organisation's principles of cash management will be determined by their specific financial regulations, guidelines and security procedures** Students need to know: • Statutory and other organisational regulations that relate to the management of cash balances • That mandatory regulations must be adhered to and awareness of these regulations should be known, as included in the Companies Act 2006 and published by HM Treasury • And have an awareness of the Money Laundering Regulations and the Bribery Act 2010

Assessment context

You need to understand the terminology in this chapter so that you can pick out key words and their meaning. You also need to be able to calculate a cash operating cycle in days.

You should also understand the role of the Government in setting monetary policies to control the supply of money.

Qualification context

You will cover working capital ratios in the Level 4 paper *Management Accounting: Decision and Control*.

Business context

If a successful business expands too quickly, it can sometimes end up with cash flow problems. This is because expanding costs money initially (investing in inventory, and debtors for example) before returns are made later.

Chapter overview

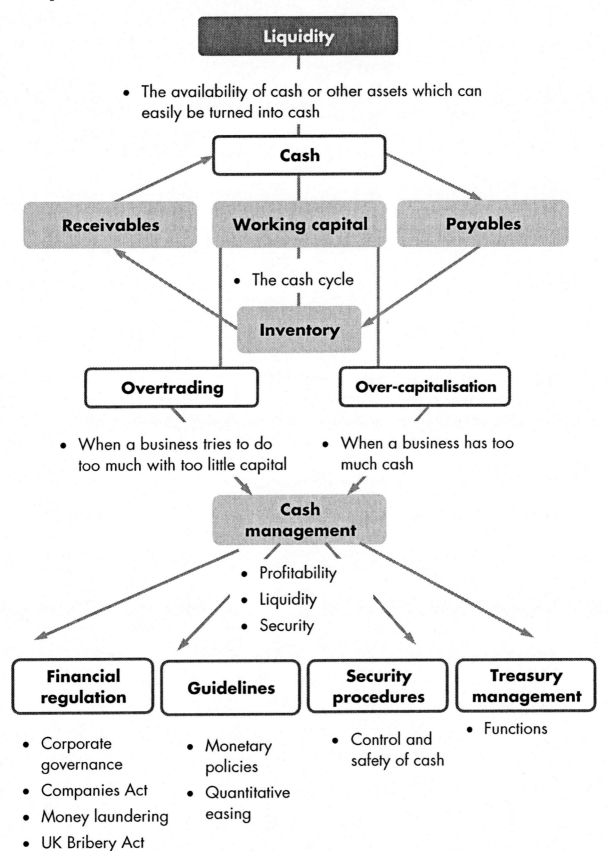

Liquidity

- The availability of cash or other assets which can easily be turned into cash

Cash

Receivables | **Working capital** | **Payables**

- The cash cycle

Inventory

Overtrading

- When a business tries to do too much with too little capital

Over-capitalisation

- When a business has too much cash

Cash management

- Profitability
- Liquidity
- Security

Financial regulation

- Corporate governance
- Companies Act
- Money laundering
- UK Bribery Act

Guidelines

- Monetary policies
- Quantitative easing

Security procedures

- Control and safety of cash

Treasury management

- Functions

Introduction

In this chapter, we consider the importance of liquidity to the success of a business and how the working capital cycle plays a part in the liquidity of the business. In the following chapters we will look at how the business can deal with a deficit or a surplus in their anticipated cash requirements.

In this chapter we examine the rules and procedures that organisations may have to follow to safeguard liquidity and to deal with cash. The chapter also considers the role of government in setting monetary policies, and other applicable rules and regulations that the business must consider when managing the movement of funds.

1 What is liquidity?

Key term

Cash Ready money, most easily thought of as banknotes and coins, and money in a current bank account. A business may be profitable but if it is unable to pay its bills, it will fail.

Liquidity The ease and speed with which an investment can be converted into cash.

Liquidity is the amount of cash a company can obtain quickly to settle its debts (and possibly to meet other unforeseen demands for cash payments too). It is the ability of a company to pay its suppliers on time, meet its operational costs such as wages and salaries and to pay any longer-term outstanding amounts such as loan repayments. Adequate liquidity is often a key factor in contributing to the success or failure of a business. The liquidity of a business depends on the availability of cash or assets which can easily be converted into cash; therefore liquidity is not just about holding cash in hand or in a bank current account, as there are also other liquid assets.

Liquid assets include:

- Cash (the most liquid)

- Short-term investments which can easily be sold and converted into cash (ie those for which there is a ready market, such as listed shares)

- Fixed-term deposits with a bank or building society – for example, six-month deposits with a bank

- Trade receivables

Liquidity is a measure of how safe the business is in terms of its cash availability. Even if a business is profitable, it must also have enough cash to pay amounts due when they become payable.

Some assets are more liquid than others. Inventories of goods are fairly liquid in some businesses. Inventories of finished production goods might be sold quickly, and a supermarket will hold consumer goods for resale that could well be sold for cash very soon. Raw materials and components in a manufacturing company have to be used to make a finished product before they can be sold to realise cash, and

BPP
LEARNING MEDIA

so they are less liquid than finished goods. Just how liquid they are depends on the speed of inventory turnover and the length of the production cycle.

Cash is the most liquid of assets and is part of the **working capital** of the business. It is also important to realise that the time taken to convert trade receivables into cash and the time taken to pay trade payables affects the liquidity position of the business.

Non-current assets are not liquid assets. A company can sell off non-current assets, but unless they are no longer needed, or are worn out and about to be replaced, they are necessary to continue the company's operations. Selling non-current assets is certainly not a long-term solution to a company's cash needs, and so although there may be an occasional non-current asset item which is about to be sold off, probably because it is going to be replaced, it is safe to disregard non-current assets when measuring a company's liquidity.

In summary, **liquid assets** are current asset items that will, or could soon, be converted into cash, and cash itself. Two common definitions of liquid assets are **all current assets** or **all current assets with the exception of inventories**.

The main source of liquid assets for a trading company is **sales**. A company can obtain cash from sources other than sales, such as the issue of shares for cash, a new loan or the sale of non-current assets. But a company cannot rely on these at all times, and in general, obtaining liquid funds depends on making sales and profits.

Activity 1: Liquid and non-liquid assets

Required

Identify examples of liquid and non-liquid assets from the following by placing a tick under the correct heading.

Solution

	Liquid assets	Non-liquid assets
Notes and coins		
Receivables		
Property		
Inventory		
Bank balance		
Short-term investments		

2 Reasons for holding cash

Cash is needed to buy resources for a business. A company is liquid if it can obtain money when it is needed. Cash is also a resource in itself, with a cost or value measurable as interest.

Activity 2: Motives for holding cash

Required

Why does a business hold cash? Give examples under each of the motives mentioned below.

Solution

Transactions motive	Precautionary motive	Speculative motive
Daily operations	Unforeseen circumstances	Opportunities
Example	Example	Example

3 Working capital

Working capital is the value of current assets less the value of current liabilities.

Key term

Current assets Cash, inventory, receivables

Current liabilities Payables, loans falling due within one year, overdraft

The two main objectives of working capital management are:

- To increase the **profits** of a business
- To provide sufficient **liquidity** to meet short-term obligations as they fall due

Activity 3: Working capital objectives

Required

How can investment in higher levels of inventory or receivables affect:

(a) Profits?
(b) Liquidity?

Solution

(a)

(b)

---

4 The cash operating cycle

There is often a **conflict** between the two main objectives of working capital management; ie management need to carefully consider the level of investment in working capital and to consider the **impact** that this is having on a company's liquidity position; an overview of this is given by the **cash operating cycle/working capital cycle**.

Cash operating cycle

The cash operating cycle is the period of time between the **outflow** of cash to pay for raw materials and the **inflow** of cash from customers.

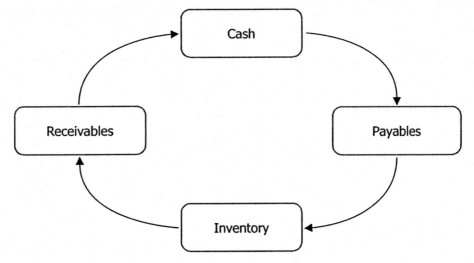

The optimal length of the cycle depends on the industry.

4.1 Calculating the cash operating cycle

Formula to learn

Average collection period	$\dfrac{\text{Receivables}}{\text{(credit) sales}}$	× 365	=	days
Inventory days	$\dfrac{\text{Inventory}}{\text{Cost of sales}}$	× 365	=	days
Average payables period	$\dfrac{\text{Payables}}{\text{(credit) purchases}}$	× 365	=	days

Cash operating cycle =

Illustration 1: Cash operating cycle

Set out below are the statement of profit or loss and statement of financial position for Hampton Manufacturing Ltd:

Hampton Manufacturing Ltd

Statement of profit or loss for the year ended 30 September 20X8

	£
Revenue	1,350,400
Cost of sales	837,200
Gross profit	513,200
Less expenses	274,000
Profit from operations	239,200

Statement of financial position as at 30 September 20X8

	£	£
Non-current assets		2,428,300
Current assets:		
Inventory	156,300	
Trade receivables	225,000	
Cash and cash equivalents	10,200	
	391,500	
Trade payables	(169,800)	
Net current assets		221,700
		2,650,000
Equity		2,000,000
Retained earnings		650,000
		2,650,000

We will now calculate the individual working capital ratios.

Inventory holding period $= \dfrac{\text{Inventory}}{\text{Cost of sales}} \times 365$

$= \dfrac{£156,300}{£837,200} \times 365$

$= 68$ days

Trade receivables' collection period $= \dfrac{\text{Trade receivables}}{\text{Credit sales}} \times 365$

$= \dfrac{£225,000}{£1,350,400} \times 365$

$= 61$ days

Trade payables' payment period $= \dfrac{\text{Trade payables}}{\text{Cost of sales}} \times 365$

$= \dfrac{£169,800}{£837,200} \times 365$

$= 74$ days

Using ratios in this way to assess the working capital cycle has certain limitations:

- Figures extracted from the statement of financial position are a snapshot of a single point in time and may not be representative of the normal level of investment in working capital eg due to seasonal fluctuations. Also, the working capital needs of a business will fluctuate with changes in the level or nature of its business activities.

- The appropriate level of working capital will vary from business to business, eg a retailer making mainly cash sales would be expected to have a low trade receivables balance, whereas a manufacturer of aeroplanes would have a high working capital requirement because of the length of the production period.

Nevertheless, considering the working capital cycle is a useful starting point in the management of cash.

For Hampton, the length of the cash operating cycle is as follows:

	Days
Inventory holding period	68
Trade receivables' collection period	61
	129
Less trade payables' payment period	(74)
Cash operating cycle	55

Therefore, 55 days elapses between Hampton paying for its raw materials and then getting cash in from the customer who has purchased the goods that these materials have been made into.

Activity 4: Cash operating cycle

The table below gives information extracted from the annual accounts of Management Co for the past year.

Management Co – Extracts from annual accounts

	Year 1 £
Inventory	270,000
Purchases of raw materials	518,400
Cost of production	675,000
Cost of goods sold	756,000
Sales	864,000
Receivables	172,800
Payables	86,400

Required

Calculate the length of the cash operating cycle (assuming 365 days in the year).

Solution

Average collection period	$\dfrac{\text{Receivables}}{\text{(credit) sales}}$	× 365	=	days
Inventory days	$\dfrac{\text{Inventory}}{\text{Cost of sales}}$	× 365	=	days
Average payables period	$\dfrac{\text{Payables}}{\text{(credit) purchases}}$	× 365	=	(days)
	Cash operating cycle =			

By comparing the cash operating cycle from one period to the next, or one company to another, it should be possible to identify potential problems.

A **lengthening** of the cash operating cycle, with more inventory and receivables or fewer payables, will **slow down** cash receipts.

A **shorter** cash operating cycle, with less inventory and receivables or more payables, will **speed up** a company's cash receipts and should improve its cash balances.

Is there an **optimum cash cycle length**? The answer will depend upon the following:

- Whether the cash cycle is too long, and investment in working capital should be reduced by shortening the cycle; or

- Whether the cash cycle is too short and becoming unsustainable, indicating a need at some time in the future for an increase in working capital investment.

5 Objectives of cash management

For this unit, we are concerned principally with cash management.

There are three main objectives to be balanced in the management of cash and liquid assets:

- Profitability
- Liquidity
- Security

In the context of cash management, **profitability** relates specifically to how the firm manages its cash in order to minimise costs and maintain a return.

A key profitability ratio is **return on capital employed (ROCE)**. This ratio expresses the profit of a company in relation to the capital employed to generate it. Note in the formula below capital employed includes not only total equity but also non-current liabilities, for example long-term bank loans. It is not uncommon though for companies to use short-term finance, such as revolving overdrafts, as part of their long-term financing needs and in some instances this can be considered as part of the capital employed in the business.

Trends are important when looking at return on capital employed. If a company has a decreasing percentage return this indicates not only a lack of printability but also an ineffective use of capital resources. Comparisons can be useful when comparing companies within the same industry who have similar capital requirements.

Formula to learn

Return on capital employed =

$$\frac{\text{Profit from operations}}{\text{Total equity + Non-current liabilities}} \times 100 = X\%$$

A **backward calculation** can also be completed. Before investors invest in a company they may be looking for a specific hurdle rate for return on capital employed before making an investment. For example, if a 20% return on capital employed is required and profit from operations are currently £100,000 then capital employed in the business would need to be kept below £500,000. To meet at least a 20% return on capital employed the backward calculation would be £100,000/0.20 = £500,000.

Security is the principle that cash and credit transactions should not involve the company in any undue risk.

Security can include physical security of assets:

- Notes and coins should be secure from theft.
- Cheques and electronic systems should be secure from fraud.
- Property and other assets should be protected from theft and damage.

Security also includes the risk of loss.

Short-term investments should be such that the firm does not stand to risk heavy losses through falls in value. Shares can fall in price.

However, there is a relationship between risk and return which a business needs to consider. Generally speaking, safer investments offer lower returns, and safer loans (such as where the borrower offers security) are charged at lower interest rates. How much risk a business is willing to take on should be a decision made by the leadership of the organisation.

6 Overtrading and over-capitalisation

Key term

> **Overtrading** Occurs when a business tries to do too much too quickly with too little long-term capital
>
> **Over-capitalisation** Occurs when a business has excessive working capital and hence is inefficient and less profitable (customers taking too long to pay, too much inventory, insufficient credit from suppliers)

Symptoms of overtrading:

- Rapid rise in sales revenue
- Rapid increase in volume of current assets
- Only a relatively small increase in proprietors' capital
- Lower liquidity/current ratios

The two overall liquidity ratios are especially important here:

> **Formula to learn**
>
> **Current ratio** = Current assets / Current liabilities
>
> **Quick ratio** or **Acid test ratio** = (Current assets – inventory) / Current liabilities

If a business has current assets of £400,000 and current liabilities of £200,000 then the current ratio can be expressed as 2:1, meaning there are £2 worth of current assets to every £1 of current liabilities. A **backward calculation** can also be completed. If a company wishes to operate on a current ratio of 2:1 and current assets are £500,000 then management will need to plan to keep current liabilities below £250,000 to maintain the 2 for 1 ratio.

Remember that the acceptable level of a ratio is dependent upon the type of business.

A key problem is that a business could easily run into liquidity problems ie not have enough capital to provide the cash to pay its debts as they fall due.

Possible actions to reduce the risk of overtrading include:

- Effective debt management and credit control
- Improving inventory control
- Making maximum use of supplier credit lines
- Focusing on cash management
- Maintaining tight control of costs
- Leasing non-current assets (rather than outright purchase)
- Capital injections or the reduction of dividends/drawings

Activity 5: Over-capitalisation

Required

What are the consequences of investing excessive cash in working capital ie over-capitalisation?

Solution

7 Organisational rules and procedures

7.1 Governance

Corporate governance is the system by which organisations are directed and controlled.

Governance is an issue for all corporate bodies, commercial and not for profit, including public sector and non-governmental organisations.

Large quoted companies generally have more stringent requirements, from both the legislative environment and the stock market on which they are listed. Each exchange has its own particular listing requirements; some are more stringent than others.

7.2 Fiduciary duty

Fiduciary duty is a duty of care and trust which one person or entity owes to another. It can be a legal or ethical obligation.

Under English law, company directors owe a fiduciary duty to the company to exercise their powers *bona fide* (in good faith) in what they honestly consider to be the best interests of the company. This duty is owed to the company and not generally to individual shareholders.

7.3 Public sector

Public sector organisations are organisations that are controlled by one or more parts of the state. Their functions are often to implement government policy.

Some are supervised by **government departments** (for example, hospitals or schools). Others are devolved bodies such as local authorities and nationalised companies (majority or all of the shares owned by the Government).

The **UK Nolan Committee on Standards in Public Life** (1995) commented that holders of public office are accountable for their decisions and actions to the public, and must submit themselves to whatever scrutiny is appropriate for their office.

The Treasury is the UK's economics and finance ministry and so it maintains control over public spending, sets the direction of the UK's economic policy and works to achieve strong and sustainable economic growth.

The Public Accounts Committee provides oversight on public spending in the UK and it focuses on value for money criteria which are based on economy, effectiveness and efficiency.

7.4 Companies Act

The Companies Act 2006 is the legal framework surrounding companies to help them do business. Their main purpose is to create wealth for the shareholders.

The Act provides directors with a list of issues to keep in mind with respect to modern day expectations of responsible business behaviour; for example, the interests of the company's employees and the impact of the company's operations on the community and the environment should be considered by directors when making decisions.

7.5 Money laundering regulations

There are extensive regulations to prevent money laundering that have been made following the **Proceeds of Crime Act 2002**, particularly the **Money Laundering Regulations 2007**.

The **Proceeds of Crime Act 2002** lists three money laundering offences:

- **Section 327** – It is an offence to hide the proceeds of crime or move it overseas. This also applies to suspicious transactions where the offender should reasonably have suspected the proceeds as originating in crime.

- **Section 328** – It is an offence to be part of any arrangement that allows others to access criminal property even if that person only suspects it to be criminal property.

- **Section 329** – It is an offence to acquire property which is known or suspected to represent the proceeds of crime.

7.6 UK Bribery Act 2010

The key points of the UK Bribery Act 2010 are as follows:

- Bribery is an intention to **encourage or induce improper performance** by any person, in breach of any duty or expectation of trust or impartiality.

- Bribery may well be treated as an offence for the **giver** ('active bribery') and the **receiver** ('passive bribery').

- Improper performance will be judged in relation to what a **reasonable person** in the UK would interpret as improper – this means instances are tested on a case by case basis in the courts. This applies even if no part of the activity took place in the UK and/or it took place where bribes may be considered standard practice locally.

- **Reasonable hospitality** (eg a business lunch) is not prohibited.

- Bribing a **foreign public official** is an offence.

- If businesses **fail to prevent** bribes being paid on their behalf, they have committed an offence punishable by an unlimited fine. **'Adequate procedures'** therefore need to be in place and shown to be operating in the business.

- Any director, manager or similar officer of an offending business **will also be guilty** of the offence if they **consented or were involved**.

Activity 6: Private and public sector cash management

Required

How does cash management differ in public and private sectors? Tick the correct statement(s) below.

Solution

	✓
Private sector is regulated by the Companies Act so any surplus cash can be invested as directors and shareholders wish, providing it is legal.	
Private sector is regulated by the Companies Act, so any surplus cash can be invested as all stakeholders wish, providing it is legal.	
Public sector is funded through public money and therefore money is only allocated where required. Any surplus should only be invested in schemes approved by central government.	
Public sector is funded through public money and therefore money is only allocated where required. Any surplus must be returned back to the taxpayers through tax breaks and tax cuts.	

8 Treasury function

In larger organisations, there is likely to be a separate **treasury function** which is responsible for dealing with liquidity management and the investment of funds.

It ensures that minimum requirements for liquidity in the organisation are met and that any investments are within the organisation's rules and regulations and offer the best return/risk/liquidity available.

Activity 7: Centralised treasury function

Required

What are the advantages of having a centralised treasury function?

Solution

9 Security procedures for dealing with cash

Cash is a highly risky asset to be holding on the business premises, as it can easily be misappropriated or stolen.

Any business dealing with cash must have basic security procedures in place to deal with the following aspects:

- **Physical safeguards** – lock and key, authorised personnel to handle cash

- **Checking for valid payment** – notes are not forged, cheques with a valid cheque guarantee card, debit and credit card payment authorisation if exceeding limit

- **Reconciliation of cash received** – with cash in till, cash box or safe, responsible official to perform reconciliation

- **Banking procedures** – bank daily or leave cash in a locked safe overnight

- **Recording procedures** – paying-in slip for the bank should not be prepared by same person doing the banking

10 Government monetary policy

Government monetary policies are the policies that are implemented by the Treasury and the Bank of England in order to deal with the supply of money, interest rates and the availability of credit.

The way in which the Government influences the amount of money in the economy is by either restricting or encouraging bank lending.

One way of doing this is by the issue of gilts. By selling attractively priced gilts, the Government takes money away from financial institutions and individuals who pay for these gilts out of their bank accounts, thereby reducing the amount that the banks can lend.

The use of Treasury bills by the Government also controls bank lending and influences the interest rate. Through the buying and selling process, the Government affects the supply and demand levels for investments generally and thereby influences interest rates.

10.1 Inflation and interest rates

Inflation is a rise in the general level of prices of goods and services in the economy and a fall in the purchasing value of money.

The main measure of inflation in the UK used by the Government is the Consumer Price Index. This calculates the average price increase as a percentage for a basket of 600 different goods and services.

High inflation rates are considered harmful to the economy and so inflation needs to be controlled. In the UK, inflation is controlled by the Bank of England's Monetary Policy Committee by setting interest rates in line with the Government's inflation target.

Changes in interest rates affect the overall demand for goods and services in the economy and, in turn, have an impact on inflation. A fall in interest rates will boost demand. This, in turn, leads to increases in prices and the inflation rate. The opposite applies with an increase in interest rates.

Higher interest rates make investment more attractive, but reduces the demand for borrowing. When interest rates are rising, investors who have taken out fixed interest investments will suffer as they are unable to take advantage of the increasing returns available. Conversely, when interest rates are falling, fixed interest investments protect the return available to investors.

10.2 Quantitative easing

Key term

Quantitative easing In a recession, the Government can lower interest rates to encourage people and businesses to spend, rather than save, and thereby increase economic growth.

However, when interest rates can go no lower, the Government has to directly pump money into the economy. This is called quantitative easing, a policy whereby a government makes more money available in the economy in order to stimulate the economy.

The way the central bank does this is by buying assets (usually government bonds) using 'new' money it has printed. The financial institutions such as commercial banks and insurance companies selling the bonds will then have this 'new' money in their accounts, which boosts the money supply. This should directly stimulate lending and economic activity.

Assessment focus point

You are not required to have a detailed knowledge of economics for your assessment. However, you are expected to have a **general awareness** of the implications of **expansionary** or **contractionary** government policies and how they might affect a business. Keeping up to date with current affairs is a good way to improve your general knowledge in this area.

Chapter summary

- Liquidity is the ability of a business to meet its payments, as and when they are due.

- The most liquid asset of all is cash but other major assets which can be converted into cash may include bank deposits, investments, inventory and trade receivables.

- Working capital is made up of inventory, trade receivables and trade payables and the cash operating cycle is an important indicator of the liquidity of a business.

- A business can try to reduce its cash operating cycle by making changes to its working capital policies.

- Liquidity management or cash management is concerned with profitability, liquidity and security.

- Overtrading and over-capitalisation can both be detected by considering the working capital ratios and the cash operating cycle.

- Organisations are subject to a number of regulations, depending on their nature. Companies are subject to the Companies Act 2006; listed companies need to also abide by the regulations of the stock market on which they are listed and public bodies should follow the regulations of their governing body, such as the Treasury in the UK. Money laundering regulations and the UK Bribery Act should also be considered.

- In a business where large amounts of cash/cheques/debit and credit card payments are received from customers, procedures should be in place to ensure that the cash is physically secure, controlled and paid into the bank as soon as possible.

- Government monetary policies are the policies implemented by the Treasury and the Bank of England in order to control the supply of money, inflation, interest rates and the availability of credit.

- Much of government monetary policy is carried out through the issuing or buying of gilts and Treasury bills in order to control the money supply and interest rates.

- Quantitative easing is where a government directly makes more money available in the economy in order to stimulate growth.

Keywords

- **Cash operating cycle:** The period of time between cash being paid for raw materials and cash being received from customers for goods sold

- **Fiduciary duty:** A duty of care and trust that one person or entity owes to another

- **Government monetary policy:** Policies implemented by the Treasury and the Bank of England to deal with the supply of money, inflation, interest rates and the availability of credit

- **Inflation:** A rise in the general level of prices of goods and services in the economy and a fall in the purchasing value of money (measured by the Consumer Price Index in the UK)

- **Inventory holding period:** The amount of time that inventory is being held by a business

- **Over-capitalisation:** Where a business has surplus assets that are being under-utilised because of over-investment in working capital

- **Overtrading:** Where a business expands more quickly than its funds allow

- **Quantitative easing:** A policy whereby a government makes more money available in the economy in order to stimulate the economy

- **Return on capital employed (ROCE):** An expression of profit in relation to the capital employed by a business

- **Trade payables' payment period:** The amount of time it takes for a business to pay its trade payables

- **Trade receivables' collection period:** The amount of time that it takes for trade receivables to pay the amounts that they owe

- **Treasury function:** A department in larger organisations that is responsible for dealing with liquidity management and the investment of funds

- **Working capital:** The total of the current assets of a business less its current liabilities

1   A business had sales of £790,000 during the year and cost of sales of £593,000. Inventory at the year end was valued at £68,000, trade receivables were £102,000 and trade payables were £57,000.

   What is the cash operating cycle of the business?

	✓
30 days	
40 days	
54 days	
124 days	

2   A business has a cash operating cycle of 35 days. Its inventory holding period is 21 days and its trade receivables' collection period is 60 days.

   What is the trade payables' payment period?

	✓
25 days	
39 days	
46 days	
56 days	

3   **Select the three most liquid assets that the majority of businesses are likely to have from the list below.**

   -
   -
   -

   Picklist:

   Bank current account
   Bank deposit account
   Business computers
   Business head office
   Cash in hand
   Fleet of cars used in the business
   Inventory of finished goods
   Inventory of raw materials
   Investment in shares
   Trade receivables

4   **Which one of the following might be associated with a lengthening cash operating cycle?**

	✓
Longer inventory holding period	
Taking longer to pay suppliers	
Lower investment in working capital	
Improved debt collection	

5   **Selecting from the picklist, complete the following sentence:**

The **three** main principles of the management of liquidity are [security/ethics/type of business invested in/liquidity/management preferences/profitability].

6   **A business has high levels of current assets but only small amounts of trade payables. What is this an example of? (Tick the appropriate answer.)**

	✓
Overtrading	
Over-capitalisation	

7   **If there is a rise in the general level of inflation, what effect is this likely to have on the real return available from gilt-edged securities?**

Tick the correct answer.

	✓
Increase	
Decrease	

8   **Describe two objectives an organisation might have in managing its working capital.**

9   **Define what is meant by the term 'overtrading' and describe some of the typical symptoms.**

Raising finance

7

Learning outcomes

4.1	**Demonstrate an understanding of how an organisation can raise finance and the basic terms and conditions associated with each of these types of financing**
	Students need to know:
	• The different ways in which an organisation can raise finance
	• The different terms and conditions surrounding the various types of financing: bank loans and overdrafts, operating and finance leases, hire purchase agreements, loan stock, sale and leaseback, factoring, invoice discounting, equity shares and bonds
4.2	**Evaluate the use of financing options to fund the organisation's cash requirements on the most beneficial terms and conditions**
	Students need to be able to:
	• Determine the accounting entries for each financing option
	• Explain the effect on gearing and liquidity for each financing option
	• Calculate and explain the total cost to a business for a financing option
	• Identify the most appropriate financing option in a given situation

Assessment context

You need to be able to identify the main features of various types of financing options, as listed in the assessment criteria above, and identify the best financing option.

Qualification context

You will cover raising finance in the Level 4 paper *Management Accounting: Decision and Control*.

Business context

A business can raise finance from a range of sources and each financing option has differing terms and conditions. Organisations may have established regulations, policies and guidelines governing how finance can be raised.

Chapter overview

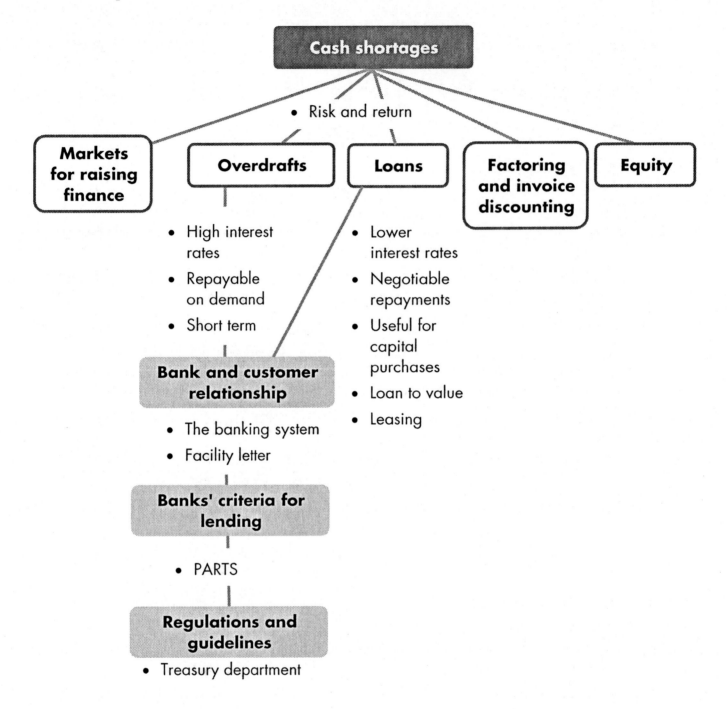

Cash shortages

- Risk and return

Markets for raising finance

Overdrafts

- High interest rates
- Repayable on demand
- Short term

Bank and customer relationship

- The banking system
- Facility letter

Banks' criteria for lending

- PARTS

Regulations and guidelines

- Treasury department

Loans

- Lower interest rates
- Negotiable repayments
- Useful for capital purchases
- Loan to value
- Leasing

Factoring and invoice discounting

Equity

Introduction

A cash budget is a useful method of determining whether it is likely that the business will have enough cash to keep going. If a **cash deficit** is forecast in the cash budget, then management will want to find suitable financing options to cover this deficit. In this chapter, we look at some of the financing options available to businesses to cover cash shortages, including a general consideration of how the banking system and **money markets** work, which is essential background information. The chapter also looks at financial **gearing** and the impact of risk on the cost of capital.

1 Cash shortages

The cash budget enables a business to anticipate future cash shortages. Management can then arrange suitable financing options to cover the cash shortages. For example, finance can be raised from banks in the form of **overdrafts** and **loans**.

There are a number of reasons why a business may need additional finance. A company must **match** the situation with an appropriate financing option.

Why we need additional finance	Appropriate ways of meeting these needs
• Short-term deficit ie support for working capital	• Overdraft • Short-term loan
• Long-term deficit	• Debt via long-term loan or debentures • Equity share capital

For the purposes of this syllabus, it is important that you appreciate:

- The various forms of finance that are available to deal with a cash deficit
- How to determine the most appropriate type of finance for the particular purpose

1.1 Overdraft versus bank loans

Ideally, short-term cash shortages for working capital should be financed using short-term capital such as overdrafts or short-term bank loans.

Bank loans can have different types of repayment schedule, namely:

- **Bullet repayment** – the amount borrowed is paid back at the end of the loan; only interest is paid during the loan period.

- **Balloon repayment** – during the term of the loan, small amounts of the amount borrowed are repaid along with loan interest, but the majority of the amount borrowed is repaid at the end of the term.

- **Amortising repayment** – the amount borrowed and interest are paid of over the term of the loan.

Banks require security they can use if their customer defaults on their repayments. This can be in the form of:

- **A fixed charge** – a named asset which the bank can insist is sold to repay the debt

- **A floating charge** – a class of assets the bank can insist is sold to repay the debt (for example: non-current assets, or receivables)

- **A personal guarantee** – a named individual who becomes personality liable in the event the original borrower defaults

An overdraft is generally a short-term source of finance. If however, an element of the overdraft is being used into the longer term, this element is known as a **'hardcore' overdraft**.

Activity 1: Sources of short-term finance

Required

Explain the features and advantages of the following forms of bank borrowing.

Solution

(a) Bank loan

Features	Advantages

(b) Overdraft facility

Features	Advantages

2 Interest

Interest rates may be **variable** or **fixed**, and their calculation can be on a **simple interest** ('**flat rate** interest') basis (ie interest is charged on the full **loan principal** at the start of the loan), or on a **compound interest** basis (ie interest is charged on the loan principal, plus unpaid accumulated interest).

Assessment focus point

In the assessment, you are only required to deal with simple interest but you may be required to calculate an interest rate if simple flat rate interest is to be applied monthly or daily.

Illustration 1: Comparing loans

A company needs a £15,000 loan for 2 years and has been offered the following options, both of which are to be repaid in 2 equal annual instalments:

Option 1: Flat rate of 7% – annual repayments of £8,550 on the last day of each year

Option 2: APR of 9% – annual repayments of £8,527 on the last day of each year

Which loan should it accept if it wants to minimise its interest payments?

On the face of it, Option 1 looks cheaper at 7% but it is incorrect to compare the flat rate with the APR.

To decide which is cheapest, the repayment schedules, rather than the interest rates, need to be compared:

	Total repayment	Capital	Interest
Option 1	(2 × 8,550) = £17,100	£15,000	£2,100
Option 2	(2 × 8,527) = £17,054	£15,000	£2,054

Option 2 is cheaper because in total the interest paid is only £2,054, compared to £2,100.

Note. Under Option 1, the company does pay 7% interest for the first year but the annual equivalent rate for the second year is much higher. The first loan repayment of £8,550 at the end of the first year consists of £7,500 capital and £1,050 interest. In year two, the capital outstanding at the start of the year is only £7,500, so the interest paid in year two of £1,050 equates to an annual equivalent rate of 14% (1,050/7,500).

Activity 2: Simple flat interest rates

A business has agreed with its bank to borrow £72,000 in order to purchase a machine. The loan is to be repaid in 36 equal monthly instalments of £2,540.

Required

Assuming simple flat rate interest, calculate:

- **The total interest cost**
- **The simple annual interest rate**

Solution

	Workings	£
Total repayments		
Total interest cost		
Interest cost p.a.		
Simple annual interest rate (%)		

3 Loan-to-value (LTV)

Key term

Loan-to-value ratio The interest rate will also be dependent on the loan-to-value ratio when the loan is for the purchase of an asset.

You may have seen this in the personal mortgage market, where a higher interest applies at higher loan-to-value ratios. If the company takes out a loan for 90% of the asset value, the interest rate is likely to be higher than a loan for 70% of the asset value.

This is because at a lower loan-to-value ratio, the risk to the lender of the borrower defaulting and being unable to recover their loan is also lower.

4 Leasing

Rather than buying an asset outright, using either available cash resources or borrowed funds, a business may lease an asset. Leasing has become a popular source of finance.

4.1 Two parties to a lease

Key term

Lessor Owns the asset and leases it out, so receives lease payments

Lessee Uses the asset, so makes lease payments

4.2 Types of leases

There are three main types of leases: **finance lease, operating lease** and **hire purchase agreement (HPA)**.

4.2.1 Key features of an operating lease

- Short-term rental – lessor retains most of the risks and rewards of ownership
- No initial capital outlay for lessee
- No risk of obsolescence

- Often maintained and insured by the lessor
- Off balance sheet finance
- Expensive

4.2.2 Key features of a finance lease

- Long-term rental – transfers substantially all of the risks and rewards of ownership of an asset to the lessee

- No need for initial capital outlay by lessee

- Simply an alternative source of finance

- May be cheaper

- Shown as non-current assets on the statement of financial position of lessee

- Book depreciation is charged on the asset

- The outstanding capital repayments (obligations) under the finance lease are shown as a liability on the statement of financial position (usually split between current and non-current liabilities)

- An interest element is charged as an expense in the income statement

4.2.3 Key features of a hire purchase agreement (HPA)

Here the hirer pays by instalments to lease the asset from the vendor, with an option to obtain ownership once the full amount of the contract has been paid.

A variation is a **sale and leaseback** arrangement in which a business that owns an asset agrees to sell the asset to a financial institution and lease it back on terms specified in the sale and leaseback agreement.

Sale and leaseback is attractive to a business experiencing cash flow problems because it enables the business to benefit from an immediate cash inflow, whilst retaining the use of the asset.

5 Factoring and invoice discounting

A **factoring** service may be:

Key term

> **With recourse** Where any bad debts are passed back to the entity
>
> **Without recourse** Where the factor bears any bad debts (and therefore risk) (or non-recourse)

Factoring can take any one or more of the following forms:

- **To provide finance** – typically 80% of the debt factored is advanced to the entity; the remainder is passed over when the customer settles the debt (net of an interest charge)

- **To administer the entity's sales ledger system** – the factor will maintain the ledger for a fee

- **To provide non-recourse finance** – again, for a fee, the factor will guarantee settlement of the debt, even if the customer doesn't pay

Non-financial issues to consider before making the decision to factor:

- **Customer relationship** – involving a debt factor effectively places a barrier between supplier and customer

- **Reputation** – debt factoring is often perceived as a sign of financial difficulty (ie cash flow problems)

- **Impacts on internal debt collection team** – may see this as an indication that they are not doing their jobs properly, and may be at risk of redundancy

- **Invoice discounting** – here, the entity maintains the administration of the sales ledger but sells selected invoices to the invoice discounter purely to obtain an advance of cash

6 Equity finance

Equity finance is raised through the sale of ordinary shares to investors via a new issue or a rights issue. The ordinary shareholders are then the owners of the company.

Ordinary shares have a nominal or 'face' value, typically £1 or 50p. This value times the number of shares issued is shown as **share capital** in the statement of financial position.

The market value of a quoted company's shares is the number of shares issued times the share price quoted on the stock market.

A **rights issue** provides a way of raising new share capital by means of an offer to existing shareholders, inviting them to subscribe cash for new shares in proportion to their existing holdings at a discounted price to the current market price.

A listed company can also raise equity finance through a **public offer** or a **placing** of shares with a large financial institution.

Usually, these methods will be used as a way of refinancing or to finance growth. These methods of issuing shares will dilute the ownership of the existing shareholders. They can also be more expensive as a method of raising equity finance than a rights issue, as the new issues can incur costs of advertising and appointing a registrar to manage the issue.

Assessment focus point

In the assessment you may need to outline the **advantages** and **disadvantages** of different methods of financing. For example, an advantage of issuing ordinary share capital is that there is no legal requirement for a company to pay a dividend or to return raised capital to shareholders. This can be compared to loan finance where there is a legal obligation to pay interest to the lender and also to repay the amount borrowed on a predetermined date.

Always adopt an effective layout for your written answers by using headings for different methods of financing and lists to clearly show your suggestions for advantages and disadvantages.

7 Risk and the cost of capital

The cost of capital has three elements:

- **Risk-free rate of return**

  This is the return which would be required from an investment if it were completely free from risk. Typically, a risk-free yield would be the yield on government securities.

- **Premium for business risk**

  This is an increase in the required rate of return due to the existence of uncertainty about the future and about a firm's business prospects.

  Business risk will be higher for some firms than for others, and some types of project undertaken by a firm may be riskier than other types of project that it undertakes.

- **Premium for financial risk**

  This relates to the danger of high debt levels (high gearing).

  The higher the gearing of a company's capital structure, the greater will be the financial risk to ordinary shareholders, as interest on debt is compulsory cash flow whereas dividends are discretionary cash flow.

  This financial risk should be reflected in a higher risk premium and therefore a higher cost of capital.

Different companies are in different types of business, so have varying **business risk**, and have different capital structures, so varying **financial risk**. Hence, no two companies will have exactly the same cost of capital.

7.1 Financial gearing

Financial gearing in a business is a measure of financial risk. It can be calculated using either of the following definitions:

Formula to learn

$$\frac{\text{Long-term debt}}{\text{Equity (includes reserves)}}$$

or

$$\frac{\text{Long-term debt}}{\text{Total capital employed ie long-term debt + equity}}$$

With the first definition: the company is highly geared if the ratio is over 100% ie high financial risk for shareholders.

With the second definition: a company is neutrally geared if the ratio is 50%, low geared below 50%, and highly geared above 50%.

A high gearing ratio also affects the credit rating of the company and its ability to borrow in the future at competitive interest rates.

Often 'long terms debt' is stated as **prior charge capital** which refers to all finance that has a right to a return before ordinary shareholders. Prior charge capital would include, for example, preference share capital.

8 The banking system

If a business is to raise additional funds externally, or invest surplus funds, then this will be done either through a bank or within the money markets. Therefore, we will now look at an overview of the banking system in the UK and the money markets.

8.1 Banks

There are two main types of banks in the UK, primary and secondary banks.

Primary banks are those which operate the money transmission service in the economy. This means that they are the banks which operate cheque accounts and deal with cheque clearing. Increasingly, they provide internet and electronic payment services as the use of cheques decreases. They are sometimes also known as the commercial, retail or clearing banks.

The **secondary banks** are made up of a wide range of merchant banks, other British banks and foreign banks in the UK. They do not tend to take part in the clearing system.

8.2 Financial intermediation

Banks take deposits from customers and then use those funds to lend money to other customers. This process is known as **financial intermediation**. The banks act effectively as middlemen, using the deposits made by savers to provide funds for those who want loans.

The main benefits of financial intermediation are as follows:

- Small amounts deposited by savers can be combined to provide larger loan packages to businesses.

- Short-term savings can be transferred into long-term borrowings.

- Search costs are reduced as companies seeking loan finance can approach a bank directly, rather than finding individuals to lend to them.

- Risk is reduced as an individual's savings are not tied up with one individual borrower directly.

8.3 Assets of banks

When individuals or companies pay money into their accounts with a bank, then the bank, of course, has that money as an asset. However, the assets of a retail bank come in a variety of different forms:

- **Notes and coins**. Branches require notes and coins to meet demands for withdrawals by customers.

- **Balances with the Bank of England**. There are two types of such balances – cash ratio deposits and operational deposits. The cash ratio deposit is a requirement of the Bank of England that a certain percentage of a bank's deposits must be held with the Bank of England. Operational deposits are the funds required to meet each bank's obligations under the clearing system for cheque payments.

- **Bills**. The banks will tend to hold very low risk bills. These include the following:
    - Treasury bills – three-month loans issued by the Bank of England on behalf of the Government
    - Local authority bills which are similar to Treasury bills but are issued by local government
    - Commercial bills of exchange which are a promise by one firm to pay another a stated amount on a certain day

- **Loans to customers** and overdrafts of customers.

- **Loans to the money markets** or other banks.

- **Securities**.

8.4 Liabilities of banks

The liabilities of the banks are the amounts that customers have paid into the bank in the form of their account balances.

8.5 Relationship between the bank and the customer

When money is paid into a bank by an individual or business and an account is opened, then that individual or business becomes a customer of the bank.

The legal relationship between the bank and its customer is quite complex and there are potentially four main contractual relationships between the bank and the customer:

- The receivable/payable (debtor/creditor) relationship
- The bailor/bailee relationship
- The principal/agent relationship
- The mortgagor/mortgagee relationship

8.5.1 Receivable/payable (debtor/creditor) relationship

When the customer deposits money, the bank becomes the receivable (debtor) and the customer a payable (creditor) of the bank. If the customer's account is overdrawn, however, the bank becomes the payable and the customer the receivable.

This relationship is essentially a contract between the bank and the customer, and there are a number of essential areas in this contract:

- The bank borrows the customer's deposits and undertakes to repay them.

- The bank must receive cheques for the customer's account.

- The bank will only cease to do business with the customer with reasonable notice.

- The bank is not liable to pay until the customer demands payment.

- The customer exercises reasonable care when writing cheques.

8.5.2 Bailor/bailee relationship

This element of the relationship between customer and bank concerns the bank accepting the customer's property for storage in its safe deposit. The bank will undertake to take reasonable care to safeguard the property against loss or damage and also to redeliver it only to the customer or someone authorised by the customer.

8.5.3 Principal/agent relationship

An agent is someone who acts on behalf of another party, the principal. Within banking, the principal/agent relationship exists where, for example, the customer pays a cheque into the bank. The bank acts as an agent when, as the receiving bank, it presents the cheque for payment to the paying bank, and then pays the proceeds into the customer's account.

8.5.4 Mortgagor/mortgagee relationship

If the bank asks the customer to secure a loan with a charge over its assets, then the relationship between the two is that of mortgagor and mortgagee. If the customer does not repay the loan, then the bank has the right to sell the assets and use the proceeds to pay off the loan.

8.6 Fiduciary relationship

The bank and the customer also have a fiduciary relationship which means that the bank is expected to act with the utmost good faith in its relationship with the customer.

8.7 The duties of the bank

The bank has a number of duties to its customers, which include the following:

- It must honour a customer's cheque, provided it is correctly made out, there is no legal reason for not honouring it and the customer has enough funds or overdraft limit to cover the amount of the cheque.

- The bank must credit cash/cheques that are paid into the customer's account.

- If the customer makes a written request for repayment of funds in their account, for example, by writing a cheque, the bank must repay the amount on demand.

- The bank must comply with the customer's instructions given by direct debit mandate or standing order.

- The bank must provide a statement showing the transactions on the account within a reasonable period and provide details of the balance on the customer's account.

- The bank must respect the confidentiality of the customer's affairs unless the bank is required by law, public duty or its own interest to disclose details or where the customer gives their consent for such disclosure.

- The bank must tell the customer if there has been an attempt to forge the customer's signature on a cheque.

- The bank should use care and skill in its actions.

- The bank must provide reasonable notice if it is to close a customer's account.

8.8 Customer's duties

The customer also has duties in respect of their dealings with their bank. The two main duties are:

- To draw up cheques carefully so that fraud is not facilitated
- To tell the bank of any known forgeries

8.9 The rights of the bank

The services that the bank provides are, of course, performed as part of its business and as such, the bank has certain rights:

- To charge reasonable bank charges and commissions over and above interest
- To use the customer's money in any way provided that it is legal and morally acceptable
- To be repaid overdrawn balances on demand (although the bank will rarely enforce this)
- To be indemnified against possible losses when acting on a customer's behalf

Key term

> **Facility letter** The legal rights and duties of either a loan or an overdraft agreement are set out in a facility letter. This is a legal document which is signed by the bank and by the customer.

Activity 3: Facility letter

Required

Explain the contents of a facility letter for a loan.

Solution

	Explanation
(a) Term of the loan	
(b) Interest rate • Fixed • Variable • Capped	
(c) Repayment structure	
(d) Any security required for the loan • **Personal guarantee**	

	Explanation
• **Fixed charge**	
• **Floating charge**	
(e) Covenants attached to the loan	

9 Banks' criteria for lending

If the bank makes a loan which is not likely to be repaid, a bank's profits suffer in three ways:

- The expected interest from the loan is not earned.

- The amount advanced and not recoverable is written off as a bad debt.

- The costs of administering the account are much increased because it requires more staff and managerial attention and there may be legal costs.

From the lender's viewpoint, the interest rate charged on loan finance will normally reflect the risk associated with the loan and an assessment of a company's creditworthiness will be made.

Risk issue	Factors that will cause the interest rate to be higher
Purpose	If the lender assesses that the project is risky or is concerned about the abilities of the management team
Amount	If the amount of the loan is high relative to the financial resources of the borrower
Repayment	If repayment of capital is at the end of the loan, rather than in instalments
Time period	If the loan is for a long time period
Security	If there are no assets available against which the loan can be secured

10 Regulations and guidelines

Different organisations may have established regulations, policies and guidelines governing the sources of, and terms under which, finance can be raised.

In the **private sector**, large businesses will have a **treasury department** who will deal with liquidity management and investment of funds (we will look at this in the next chapter).

In the **public sector**, large organisations such as local authorities also operate a treasury function. It will have a set of standing orders or regulations which dictate the types of investment and borrowing that are allowed.

11 Markets for raising finance

Key term

Capital market A capital market is a market for raising long-term finance, for example a stock exchange or investing long term.

Money markets The money markets are a vast array of markets for raising short-term finance or investing in the short term.

Within the capital and money markets, there is a primary and secondary market for trading in financial instruments.

Primary market A primary market is where new financial instruments are issued for cash.

Secondary market A secondary market is where existing financial instruments are traded between investors in the market.

Local authority market The local authority market is a market where local government authorities borrow short-term funds by issuing local authority bills with a maturity of about one year or shorter.

Inter-bank market The inter-bank market is a market for very short-term borrowing, often overnight, between the banks. It is used to smooth fluctuations in the banks' receipts and payments.

London Inter-Bank Offered Rate (LIBOR) The interest rate charged in this market is the LIBOR. The individual banks then use this rate in order to set their own base rate which determines the interest rate that they will offer to their own customers.

Activity 4: Financing options

A partnership firm needs to arrange funding for expansion which will require £50,000 capital expenditure and an additional £20,000 working capital.

The partnership finance policy states that:

- Partners must take every step to minimise the interest payable by the partnership, while not exposing the partnership to unnecessary risk.

- Loan finance may be secured on the assets of the partnership.

- The maximum allowable overdraft facility is £20,000.

- Interest will be payable on funds made available to the business by the partners in excess of their fixed capital at a maximum rate of 4% p.a.

It is considering the following financing options:

- **Option 1:** A five year bank loan of £70,000 which will be secured on the assets of the partnership. £14,000 of capital is to be repaid at the end of each year. The loan will carry fixed interest at 8% on the balance outstanding at the start of each year. An arrangement fee of 0.5% of the total amount of the bank loan is payable immediately.

- **Option 2:** A loan of £15,000 by each of the five partners. The partners are able to make their own private arrangements to raise the cash but are only prepared to provide it to the business in return for receiving interest of 5% per annum until such time as the partnership is able to repay the additional funds.

- **Option 3:** A bank loan of £50,000 which will be backed by personal guarantees from the partners. Interest will be charged at 5% above the bank's base rate which is currently 2%. An arrangement fee of 1% of the loan is payable immediately. The loan principal is repayable in full at the end of five years. In addition, the business will be granted an overdraft facility of £25,000 at an interest rate of 10% p.a. The partners believe that, on average, the business will operate with an overdraft of £10,000 throughout the year but will on occasion need to use the full extent of the facility.

Required

(a) Complete the table below to compare the total cost of servicing the finance over the five years.

(b) In line with the partnership financing policy and the cost of capital, state which option will be best by filling in the blanks in the statement below.

Solution

(a) Table evaluating the best financing option:

	Arrangement fee £	Total loan interest over 5 years £	Total overdraft interest over 5 years £	Total cost of servicing finance over 5 years £	Capital repayments required £
Option 1					
Option 2					
Option 3					

(b) Decision:

Option [   ] (1/2/3) should be selected because: (Tick all statements that are valid)

	✓
It is the only option that complies with the partnership finance policy	
It is the quickest and easiest way to raise the finance	
It is the cheapest in terms of overall servicing cost	
The partnership will have sufficient funds to make the capital repayments needed	

Assessment focus point

The double entry and financial reporting treatment for the various sources of finance have been covered as part of your other studies, for example the *Financial Statements of Limited Companies* unit.

Chapter summary

- One of the primary purposes of the banking system is that of financial intermediation.

- The assets of the banks take a variety of forms including cash, deposits held with the Bank of England, bills, loans and overdrafts – the liabilities of the bank are its customers' account balances.

- There are four potential contractual relationships between a bank and its customer, with the most important being the receivable/payable (debtor/creditor) relationship.

- Not only do banks have a number of duties to their customers but the customers also have a duty to take care to ensure that fraud is not facilitated.

- The money markets are a vast array of markets, buying and selling different forms of cash and marketable securities.

- Once a forecast cash deficit is identified, the reason for the deficit must first be determined in order to identify the most appropriate source of finance.

- A cash deficit is often caused by working capital problems or by the need to fund an increasing cash cycle – in other cases, the cash deficit may be due to the need to purchase non-current assets or even acquire another business.

- Over the short term, the two main sources of additional finance are either overdraft finance or a loan.

- An overdraft facility may be granted by the bank and the business can then run an overdraft of any amount up to that facility total – interest will be charged only on the amount of the actual overdraft on a daily basis.

- If loan finance is taken out, the loan agreement or facility letter will include details of the term of the loan, the interest rate, the repayment pattern, any security and any covenants.

- The choice between an overdraft and a loan will normally depend upon the reason for the deficit – in general, a deficit due to working capital shortages will be financed by an overdraft but, if the deficit is for the purchase of longer-term non-current assets, a loan to match the life of the assets would be more appropriate.

- Some companies use factoring and invoice discounting to help short-term liquidity or to reduce administration costs.

- Leasing is a commonly used source of finance. We distinguish three types of leasing: operating leases, finance leases, and hire purchase agreements.

- Equity finance is raised through the sale of ordinary shares to investors via a new issue or a rights issue.

- The cost of capital is the rate of return that the enterprise must pay to satisfy the providers of funds, and it reflects the riskiness of providing funds.

- The creditworthiness of customers needs to be assessed by balancing the risks and costs of a customer defaulting against the profitability of the business provided by the customer.
- The gearing of an organisation is the amount of debt finance used by a company relative to its equity finance.

- **Amortising repayments:** Repayments are made up of interest and principal so that there is no principal remaining at the end of the loan term

- **Balloon repayments:** Some loan principal is paid off during the term of the loan but most of it at the end of the loan period

- **Bullet repayments:** The entire loan is paid off at the end of the loan period with only interest payments made during the term of the loan

- **Business risk:** Uncertainty about the future and about a firm's business prospects which will cause its profits before interest and tax to vary

- **Capital market:** A capital market is a market for raising long-term finance, for example a stock exchange or investing long term

- **Cash deficit:** Shortage of cash

- **Compound interest:** Interest is charged on the loan principal plus unpaid accumulated interest

- **Covenants:** Obligations or restrictions placed on the business by the loan provider

- **Facility letter:** A formal document signed by both the bank and the customer, setting out the legal rights and duties relating to loan or overdraft finance

- **Factoring:** An arrangement to have debts collected by a factor company, which advances a proportion of the money it is due to collect

- **Finance lease:** A lease that transfers substantially all of the risks and rewards of ownership of an asset to the lessee

- **Financial intermediation:** The process of banks taking deposits from customers to lend to others

- **Financial risk:** The risk to investors of increasing levels of debt finance

- **Fixed charge:** Security for the loan is a specific asset which cannot be sold without the bank's permission

- **Fixed rate interest:** An agreed fixed rate of interest for the term of a loan

- **Flat-rate interest:** The interest rate for the period of the loan is calculated based on the original loan principal

- **Floating charge:** Charge on a group of assets that are constantly changing such as receivables or inventory

- **Gearing:** The amount of debt finance a company uses relative to its equity finance

- **Hardcore overdraft:** An overdraft which has effectively become a permanent part of the capital of the business

- **Inter-bank market:** The inter-bank market is a market for very short-term borrowing, often overnight, between the banks. It is used to smooth fluctuations in the banks' receipts and payments

- **Invoice discounting:** The purchase of a selection of invoices, at a discount

- **Loan:** An amount of money advanced by a bank to its customer

- **Loan principal:** The fixed amount of capital borrowed

- **Loan-to-value:** The size of the loan in relation to the value of the asset for which the loan is being granted

- **Local authority market:** The local authority market is a market where local government authorities borrow short-term funds by issuing local authority bills with a maturity of about one year or shorter

- **London Inter-Bank Offered Rate (LIBOR):** The interest rate prevailing in the London inter-bank market

- **Money markets:** Markets buying and selling different forms of money and marketable securities

- **Operating lease:** A lease where the lessor retains most of the risks and rewards of ownership

- **Overdraft:** The amount by which a customer's bank account is in debt

- **Overdraft facility:** The amount of potential overdraft that a bank allows a customer

- **Personal guarantee:** A personal undertaking from the owner of a business that, should the business fail to make loan payments when due, the individual guarantor will pay from personal assets

- **Primary banks:** The high street or retail banks

- **Primary market:** New financial instruments are issued for cash

- **Prior charge capital:** Capital which has a right to interest or preferred dividends in precedence to any claim by the ordinary shareholders

- **Rights issue:** An offer to existing shareholders enabling them to buy more shares, usually at a price lower than the current market price

- **Risk-free rate of return:** The return which would be required from an investment if it were completely free from risk

- **Sale and leaseback:** When a business that owns an asset agrees to sell the asset to a financial institution and lease it back on terms specified in the sale and leaseback agreement

- **Secondary banks:** Banks other than the primary banks operating in the UK

- **Secondary market:** Existing financial instruments are traded between participants in the market

- **Simple interest:** Interest is charged on the loan principal

- **Variable rate interest:** Interest on a loan which changes every time the bank changes its base rate

Test your learning

1   **Which of the following is not a common contractual relationship between a bank and its customer?**

	✓
Trustee/beneficiary	
Principal/agent	
Mortgagor/mortgagee	
Bailor/bailee	

2   **Which of the following is not part of the main duties of a bank in relation to its customers?**

	✓
Honour the customer's cheque provided it is correctly made out and there are sufficient funds to pay the cheque	
Grant an overdraft when requested	
Respect the confidentiality of the customer's affairs	
Provide a statement showing the transactions on the customer's account within a reasonable period	

3   **Using the picklist, complete the following sentence.**

LIBOR stands for [lowest intra-bank operating rate/London inter-bank offered rate/London inter-bank operating rate].

4   Compare overdraft finance with that of a loan.

   Which of the following would be advantages of overdraft finance for a company seeking short-term finance?

   Tick the appropriate boxes.

	✓
Floating charge required	
Interest charged only on amount of facility used	
Repayable on demand	

5   A Ltd is considering the purchase of shares in B Ltd which will require external finance and will be held for a number of years.

What would be the most appropriate source of finance for this purchase?

	✓
Overdraft finance	
Loan finance	

6   **What are the three main repayment patterns of repaying a loan?**

   •

   •

   •

7   **Using the picklist, complete the following sentence.**

A fixed charge is security against the [non-current assets/current assets] of a business.

8   **Explain how the factoring of invoices may assist a firm's cash position.**

9   **How can a company reduce its level of gearing?**

Managing surplus funds

8

Learning outcomes

3.1	Explain how government monetary policies affect an organisation's treasury functions
	Students need to know:
	• How the government, through monetary policy, can influence the rate of inflation and the supply of money through quantitative easing
	• The main roles of the Bank of England
3.4	Discuss the role of the treasury function
	Students need to know:
	• The main roles of the treasury function in an organisation
	• The relationship between risk and return
	• How to invest surplus funds to maximise the return on the investment, with due regard to the organisation's attitude to risk
5.1	Evaluate different types of investment and the associated risk, terms and conditions
	Students need to know:
	• The various forms of investing surplus funds available to an organisation: land, property, shares, bonds, gilts, various types of bank accounts, certificates of deposit and investments in commodities
	• The different types of investment
5.2	Analyse ways to manage risk when investing to minimise potential exposure to the organisation
	Students need to know:
	• The relationship between risk, reward and liquidity when investing surplus funds
	• How to analyse the risk and return of different options
	• The most beneficial method of investment in a given situation
	• The portfolio effect of diversifying investments

5.3	Consider the investment of surplus funds according to organisational culture and policy.
	Students need to know:
	• That various investments may have a minimum investment level
	• That some investments may have conditions where withdrawal is restricted
	• How the ethics, sustainability or working practices of companies in which investments are made could affect an organisation's reputation and decision making (this will involve both inwardly looking and outwardly looking issues that could affect the company)
	• What the effect of the above restrictions could be in influencing the decision on whether or not to invest
5.4	**Evaluate economic conditions that could affect various financial markets.**
	Students need to know:
	• The benefits, advantages and disadvantages of investing in local economies versus wider economies or the global economy
	• How this could affect the treasury function's role in an organisation
	• Whether to invest surplus funds or to reduce debt due to the change in economic conditions
	• The effect of interest rates, exchange rates and commodity prices on financial markets
	• The differences between fiscal and monetary policies and how a government can attempt to use these to manage an economy

Assessment context

You need to be able to identify the features of different types of investments and recommend an option to invest surplus funds, bearing in mind the three key factors of risk, return and liquidity.

Qualification context

You will also consider managing surplus funds in the Level 4 paper *Management Accounting: Decision and Control.*

Business context

An organisation needs to be able to utilise cash surpluses in the most appropriate manner to ensure it receives maximum return for the tolerable risk.

Chapter overview

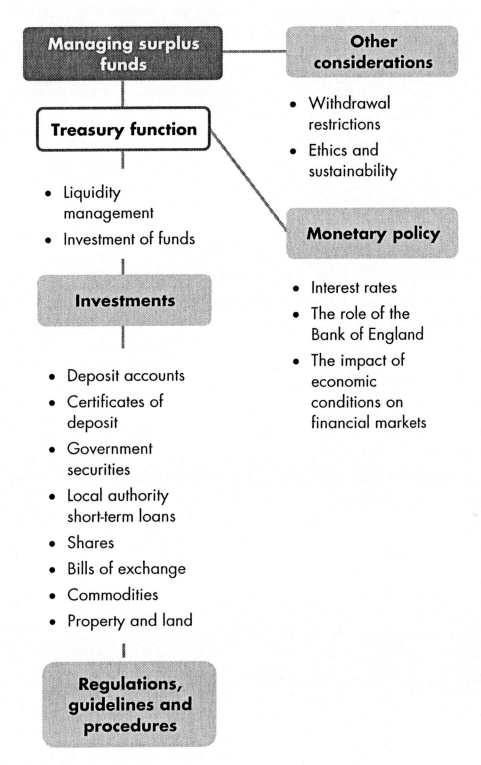

Managing surplus funds

Other considerations

- Withdrawal restrictions
- Ethics and sustainability

Treasury function

- Liquidity management
- Investment of funds

Monetary policy

- Interest rates
- The role of the Bank of England
- The impact of economic conditions on financial markets

Investments

- Deposit accounts
- Certificates of deposit
- Government securities
- Local authority short-term loans
- Shares
- Bills of exchange
- Commodities
- Property and land

Regulations, guidelines and procedures

Introduction

In a similar way to selecting suitable finance for dealing with cash shortages, organisations also need to utilise **cash surpluses** in the most appropriate manner, in order to ensure that they maximise **return** for the tolerable level of **risk**.

1 Treasury function

In larger organisations, there is likely to be a separate treasury function which is responsible for dealing with liquidity management and the investment of funds.

There are three main factors that should be considered when determining how to invest any surplus funds.

1.1 Risk

When cash is invested there are two main risks. There is the risk that the value of the investment will fall, which is the **capital risk**.

There is also the risk that the return from the investment will be lower than expected due to changes in market rates of return.

Some investors are more concerned about risk than others. Their attitude to risk is known as their **risk appetite**.

1.2 Return

The return on an investment has two potential aspects – the **income return** and the **capital return**.

Most investments will pay some form of interest or dividend which is the income return. However, many investments will also tend to fluctuate in value over time and this gives the capital return (or capital loss).

The general relationship between risk and return with investments is that the higher the risk, the higher the expected return.

1.3 Liquidity

Liquidity is the term used for the ease and speed with which an investment can be converted into cash.

1.4 Relationship between risk, return and liquidity

When a cash surplus is to be invested, the aim will be to earn a good return but without incurring excessive risk of loss and also ensuring that the investment can be realised within the timescale in which the cash is required.

Illustration 1: Risk, return and liquidity

The glass division of SC Fuel and Glass has £60,000 to invest for the next month until the money is needed to pay the quarterly sales tax (VAT) bill. It could be paid into an interest-bearing deposit account at the bank where it will earn 0.5% interest for the month. Alternatively, it could be used to buy shares in another company.

If it is paid into the deposit account then the money bears virtually no risk at all (provided that the bank is creditworthy). One month later, the money will be withdrawn and will total:

£60,000 + (60,000 × 0.005) = £60,300

The business has made a profit or return of £300 and the money is available to pay the sales tax bill.

If the shares were purchased, then it is possible that they would have increased in value to, say, £66,000 in one month's time, meaning that the glass division has earned a profit of £6,000. However, it is also possible, due to the risk of investment in shares, that the shares might have fallen in value to £55,000. This would mean that not only has the glass division made a loss of £5,000 but also the full amount of cash is not available to meet the sales tax bill.

2 Types of investments

There are many ways in which surplus funds can be invested. However, we can identify two main types:

(a) **Cash based investments:**

Bank or building society accounts – Surplus funds can be deposited in a bank or building society account. If the cash is definitely not required in the near future, then it could be invested in a deposit account for a fixed term of up to three months at a variable rate of interest which is linked to money market rates. This will give a higher rate of return.

Money market accounts – These are similar in principle to a bank deposit account. Here funds are deposited with a bank or other financial institution for a fixed period of time and cannot be accessed until the term has ended. Terms range from overnight to 12 months.

(b) **Securities** – A certificate giving evidence of a debt or equity obligation. These include property, land, shares (equity and preference, listed and private), bonds, gilts, Treasury bills, bills of exchange, certificates of deposit (CDs) and gold.

Investing is often done via a **financial intermediary**, which brings together investors and users of finance.

Key options are discussed in more detail below.

2.1 Bank or building society deposit accounts

One of the safest forms of investment for surplus cash is to pay it into a high street bank or building society deposit account. Retail banks and building societies offer a wide range of such accounts, although the interest rate, particularly for small sums, is generally quite low. Online accounts tend to attract a higher interest rate.

There are higher interest deposit accounts for larger amounts, for example provided that there is always a balance of, say, £10,000 in the account. Access to the cash is usually immediate and therefore useful if cash requirements are not known for certain.

If the cash is definitely not required in the near future, then it could be invested in a deposit account for a fixed term of up to three months at a variable rate of interest which is linked to money market rates. This will give a higher rate of return.

2.2 Money market accounts

These are similar in principle to bank deposit accounts. Here, funds are deposited with a bank or other financial institution for a fixed period of time and cannot be accessed until the term has ended. Terms range from overnight to 12 months.

2.3 Securities

2.3.1 Gilt-edged securities

Gilt-edged securities or **gilts** are marketable UK government securities. They are fixed interest securities and they form the major part of the fixed interest market. The interest rate on a gilt is also known as a **coupon rate**. Gilts are classified according to their redemption dates as follows:

- Shorts – lives up to 5 years, eg Treasury 5% 2018
- Mediums – lives from 5 to 15 years, eg Treasury 5% 2025
- Longs – lives of more than 15 years, eg Treasury 4% 2060
- Undated stocks – no redemption date
- Index-linked stocks, eg Treasury IL 2.5% 2024

A **Treasury bill** is government short-term debt, maturing in less than one year, and generally issued at a discount.

Treasury bills are issued weekly by the Government to finance short-term cash deficiencies in the Government's expenditure programme. The holder is paid the full value of the bill on maturity. Since they are negotiable, they can be resold, if required, before their maturity date.

Treasury bills do not pay interest, but the purchase price of a Treasury bill is less than its face value, the amount that the Government will eventually pay on maturity. There is thus an implied rate of interest in the price at which the bills are traded.

2.3.2 Local authority stocks

In a similar way to government securities, there are a large number of marketable local authority securities which are available for investment purposes. However,

local authority stocks are not considered to be quite as secure as central government stocks and the market is not so large, which means that local authority stocks have a slightly higher yield than government stocks to compensate.

2.3.3 Bonds

Bond is a term given to any interest-paying security, whether it be issued by the Government, a company, a bank or other institution. (Gilts are therefore UK government bonds.) Businesses also issue bonds. They are usually for the long term, and usually pay a fixed rate of interest. They may or may not be secured.

2.3.4 Certificate of deposit (CD)

A **CD** is a document issued by a bank or building society which certifies that a certain sum, usually a minimum of £50,000, has been deposited with it, to be repaid on a specific date. The term can range from seven days to five years but is usually for six months.

CDs are negotiable instruments which means that they can be bought and sold. Therefore, if the holder does not want to wait until the maturity date, the CD can be sold in the money market.

CDs offer a good rate of interest, are highly marketable and can be liquidated at any time at the current market rate. The market in CDs is large and active, therefore they are an ideal method for investing large cash surpluses.

2.3.5 Bills of exchange

A **bill of exchange** can be defined as an unconditional order in writing from one person to another, requiring the person to whom it is addressed to pay a specified sum of money, either on demand (a **sight bill**) or at some future date (a **term bill**) *(Bills of Exchange Act, 1882)*. A cheque is a special example of a type of bill of exchange.

Most bills of exchange are term bills with a duration or maturity of between two weeks and six months and are of a value of up to £500,000 in any currency. If one company draws a bill on another company, this is known as a trade bill. However, the market in these is small.

Most bills are **bank bills**, which are bills of exchange drawn and payable by a bank; the most common of these is known as a banker's acceptance. There is an active market in such bills and a company with surplus cash could buy a bill of exchange at a discount and either hold it to maturity or sell it in the market before maturity again at a discount. The difference between the price at which the bill is purchased and the price at which it is sold or it matures is the return to the investor.

2.3.6 Commodities (for example gold)

Commodities are physical products such as gold. They are traded on commodity exchanges where standard contracts are bought and sold.

While gold and other precious metals are the best known commodities, other products are also traded, including food, energy and minerals.

In addition to the contract for the commodities, more complex financial instruments (derivatives) have been developed, such as forward contracts where a price is set today for an exchange that will take place at a set date in the future.

Some commodities, such as gold, are seen as a safe investment because they retain value in times of uncertainty in the financial markets. Other commodities, such as food, can be seen as more of a speculative investment as the yield from a harvest in any single year can be variable and the price of food can fluctuate quite significantly according to the yield.

2.3.7 Equity

An **equity** investment is generally the purchase of shares in another company. Often this takes place through a stock market. Income is from dividend payments and capital gains on the increase in the share value.

Formula to learn

The dividend yield from an equity investment can be calculated as follows:

$$\frac{\text{Annual dividend}}{\text{Current share price}} \times 100$$

Dividend yield shows the dividend payments made to shareholders, however it is common practice for companies not to pay out all their earnings as dividends and to retain some profit for reinvestment into the business. These earnings that are retained may be used to purchase non-current assets or to provide a cushion of cash for any lean times ahead.

Some investors prefer to use an alternative measurement so that all earnings are included in their yield calculation. This is called the earnings yield.

Formula to learn

The earnings yield from an equity investment can be calculated as follows:

$$\frac{\text{Annual earnings}}{\text{Current share price}} \times 100$$

A **backward calculation** can also be completed. If an investor is looking for an 8% earnings yield on their investment and current annual earnings are £0.50 per share the investor may only be willing to pay £6.25 per each share purchased. To meet the 8% earnings yield required the backward calculation would be (£0.50/0.08) × 100 = £6.25.

Both the dividend yield and earnings yield are useful to investors as they enable comparisons between companies and also the return from available current interest rates.

Investments in companies that are traded on a stock exchange are very easily sold, so these are a relatively liquid form of investment. However, unless the investment is a speculative one, in anticipation of a rapid increase in the company's value, investments in equity are normally held for longer periods.

2.3.8 Property and land

Investing in property and land is generally a very safe investment. However, the costs of maintaining and generating an income from property and land are higher than for other forms of investment.

These are generally long-term investments due to the costs and time associated with purchasing and selling land and property.

Assessment focus point

When answering written questions involving investment in property and land, always take **liquidity** into consideration. It can take many months of negotiation and legal work to sell property or land so this type of investment is more suited to the longer term and not for investors who may need to 'cash in' their investment at short notice. Although property and land normally have an upward trend in market price over the years, there is always the **risk** that when the time to sell comes, the price achieved may not be as high as hoped for.

Activity 1: Investment types

Required

Explain the nature of the following investments and the risks, costs, terms and conditions associated with them.

Solution

	Short term or long term?	Explanation
Certificates of deposit		
Government securities: • Treasury bills • Gilts		
Local authority deposits		
Shares		

3 Diversification

Holding more than one different investment always carries less risk than holding only one. If only one investment is held, the investor could lose a lot if this one investment fails. The extent to which risk can be reduced will depend on the relationship which exists between the different returns.

The process of reducing risk by increasing the number of separate investments in a portfolio is known as **diversification**.

A business should aim to create a diversified portfolio of investments, with a spread of risk and return. Marketable UK securities can be ranked in order of increasing risk and increasing expected return.

- Government securities
- Local authority stocks
- Other 'public' corporation stocks
- Company loan stocks
- Other secured loans
- Unsecured loans
- Convertible loan stocks
- Preference shares
- Equities

Low risk

High risk

4 Monetary policy

The Government's monetary policy can impact an organisation's treasury function.

Monetary policies are implemented by the Bank of England in order to deal with the supply of money, interest rates and the availability of credit. The object of monetary policy is to maintain **price stability**. Low inflation can help to achieve sustainable long-term economic growth.

As an alternative or complement to monetary policy, **fiscal policy** can be used by governments. Fiscal policy is the balance between **government spending** and **taxation**. If the Government increases spending and/or reduces taxation, this is known as an **expansionary** fiscal policy. This **increases** demand (as more money is in the trading economy) which **stimulates** the economy. Alternatively, if the Government **decreases spending** and/or **increases taxation**, this is known as a **contractionary** fiscal policy. This **decreases** demand (as less money is in the trading economy) which **slows the economy down**.

In the execution of monetary policy, the Bank of England sets short-term interest rates which affect the whole pattern of rates set by banks.

When interest rates are increased, this reduces the demand for borrowing. This, in turn, has the effect of reducing consumer demand as less credit is available and the credit that is available is too costly.

4.1 The Bank of England

The Bank of England has two key roles in the economy:

- Carrying out **monetary policy** by setting the base rate of **interest** to control the level of inflation in the economy. The base rate of interest sets the basis for most other interest rates in the economy. High interest rates mean higher borrowing costs for businesses, and lower demand as customers prefer to save. The Bank of England also controls the degree of **quantitative easing** in the economy (see Chapter 6).

- Ensuring **financial stability**. The **Financial Policy Committee (FPC)** of the Bank of England monitors risks to the economy and recommends a course of action to reduce risks (for example in the UK, one risk is accelerating house price growth). The Bank of England also manages the **Prudential Regulation Authority (PRA)** which supervises the financial sector of the economy and protects the general public from excessive risk taking.

5 Regulations, guidelines and procedures

Different organisations will have their own financial regulations, guidelines and security procedures that must be observed when making decisions on the management of surplus funds.

A large business in the private sector may have regulations which set out:

- The types of investment that are allowed
- A minimum requirement for highly liquid funds
- Who is responsible for liquidity management and up to what limit

6 Other considerations for investing surplus cash

The decision of what to invest surplus funds in is primarily one that considers risk, liquidity and return. However, there are other factors in addition to this.

6.1 Minimum level and withdrawal restrictions

Some investments require a minimum amount to be invested. For example, a money market bank deposit or a CD may require an investment of at least £50,000. This may well influence the choice of where to invest the funds, especially if a partial withdrawal is anticipated that reduces the investment to below the minimum level.

In some cases, partial or pre-term withdrawals are either not permitted or heavily penalised – for example with a fixed-term bank deposit. This should be considered when formulating policy about investing surplus funds as their liquidity could be drastically reduced.

6.2 Ethics, sustainability and working practices

Ethics concerns issues of **morality** – right and wrong. Performing **sustainably** means not working in a way that compromises the future performance. The decision to invest surplus funds should consider both these aspects. Failure to consider them could result in:

- **Internally focused issues**: Investing in an immoral or unsustainable way (for example in a business or location involved in extreme worker exploitation). This could affect workers' morale and damage productivity and culture.

- **Externally focused issues**: Investing in an immoral or unsustainable way could have a detrimental effect on wider stakeholder relationships. For example, should they find out about the unethical/unsustainable investments the business could lose customers, suppliers, future providers of finance and existing investors – all of which will be ultimately detrimental to the performance of the business.

7 The impact of economic conditions on financial markets

7.1 Local or overseas investment?

Investing surplus funds in the local economy has various **advantages**:

- Better **knowledge** of the local market
- Fewer **language** issues
- Familiar **legal system** and **economy**
- Often **quicker** implementation of decisions
- **No foreign exchange** management issues

However, investing more internationally affords the benefit of **diversification**. Should the local economy suffer for a local reason, the overseas investment is less likely to be affected. In addition, the overseas market may be inherently **more stable** or **profitable** than the local one, depending on location.

7.2 Impact on the treasury function's role

If the business's policy is to invest surplus funds overseas, the treasury department is likely to be more involved than otherwise, for example:

- Researching **alternatives** including assessing risk, return and liquidity

- **Managing exchange rate risk** from an overall perspective (known as 'hedging')

- Arranging for overseas **transfers**

7.3 Impact of economic conditions

Financial markets are affected by various economic factors, including:

- **Interest rates**: If they increase, this makes funding more expensive for businesses, and demand lower from customers.

- **Exchange rates**: If they strengthen, the local currency becomes more valuable (a move from, say, $2:£1 to $2.50:£1). This discourages investment in the UK as it is expensive to send money to the UK. It also makes exports worth less sterling, but imports become cheaper. Even if a business doesn't trade overseas, it is still affected by exchange rates, as they affect raw material prices and the price of competitors' imports.

- **Commodity prices** (for example oil, gold): If they rise then costs for businesses rise, resulting in increased prices generally. Oil for example is a pervasive substance – it affects the price of anything that involves transportation, the use of plastic, or the use of energy.

These factors in turn affect the performance of individual businesses.

Assessment focus point

When answering written questions look out for information on interest rates. As an example, when interest rates are **high** this can encourage investment in interest paying accounts. This will take money from other types of investments such as shares, where dividend returns may not seem as attractive when compared to returns elsewhere.

Activity 2: Investing surplus funds

DogsRus has £60,000 to invest for the next month until the money is needed to pay the quarterly VAT bill.

Required

Recommend how these surplus funds should be invested, taking into account the key factors.

Solution

Activity 3: Evaluating investment options

A company has an investment policy which specifies the following:

- Investments must be medium-low risk.
- The maximum to be invested in a single investment is £50,000.
- The minimum required return is 3% p.a.
- An investment must be convertible into cash within one month.

The company has £100,000 to invest and is considering the following options.

Option 1:

Minimum investment £60,000, interest rate 3.9% p.a., 30-day notice period, the majority of the investment is held in treasury stock, with a small amount in shares of FTSE 100 quoted companies.

Option 2:

No minimum investment, interest rate 3% p.a., investment in gilts.

Option 3:

Minimum investment £50,000, bank deposit account, interest rate 3.5% p.a., 30-day notice period.

Option 4:

No minimum investment, investment in portfolio of shares in quoted companies, interest rate 4.5% p.a., and no notice period.

Required

(a) **Complete the table below to assess whether the investment options comply with the company's investment policy:**

Investment policy criteria	Risk High/Med/Low	Within investment limit Yes/No	Annual return %	Liquidity acceptable (1 month conversion) Yes/No
Option 1				
Option 2				
Option 3				
Option 4				

(b) **Complete the gap fills to recommend an appropriate investment strategy for the company, showing the investments in order of preference.**

	Recommended option (insert number)	Amount invested £	Total return £
Preferred option			
Next best option			
Total			

(c) **Overall the company will earn a [　　] % return on its investment.**

Assessment focus point

In your assessment you could be asked to consider the options for investing surplus cash. Consider first the three requirements of risk, return and liquidity to help assess your options.

Chapter summary

- An organisation's financial strategy will underpin its financial decisions.

- Treasury management is a significant function within larger organisations and the treasurer must consider the risk, return and liquidity needs of the organisation.

- If a cash surplus is identified, then it should normally be invested to earn profits for the business – when considering potential investments thought should be given to risk, return and liquidity.

- There are many types of investment that would be suitable for surplus cash. These include bank deposit accounts, gilt-edged securities, local authority stocks, certificates of deposit, bills of exchange, commodities, property and land and equities.

- The relative attractiveness of investing in any of these securities derives from their return and the risk. Both of these are affected by a government's monetary policy as carried out by the Bank of England.

- Businesses should have guidelines in place covering what sort of investments are allowed and how much should be invested in lower risk securities. Ethics and sustainability issues should be considered in the formulation of these policies.

- Diversification across a range of separate investments can reduce risk for the investor.

- **Bank bill:** Bill of exchange drawn and payable by a bank

- **Bill of exchange:** Unconditional order in writing from one person to another requiring the person to whom it is addressed to pay a specified sum

- **Bond:** Any debt security, whether it be issued by the Government, a company, a bank or other institution

- **Capital return:** Increase/decrease in market value of an investment

- **Capital risk:** The risk that the value of an investment will fall

- **Cash surplus:** Surplus cash held in the business's current account

- **Certificate of deposit:** A document issued by a bank which certifies that a certain sum has been deposited with it to be repaid on a specific date – a negotiable instrument and highly marketable

- **Commodities:** Physical products such as gold, traded on commodity exchanges

- **Coupon rate:** Interest rate included in the title of gilts

- **Diversification:** The process of reducing risk by increasing the number of separate investments in a portfolio

- **Equity:** Investment in the shares of another company

- **Financial intermediary:** An institution bringing together providers and users of finance

- **Gilt-edged securities/gilts:** Marketable UK government securities

- **Income return:** Interest or dividend received

- **Liquidity:** The ease and speed with which an investment can be converted into cash

- **Local authority stocks:** Marketable local authority securities which have a higher yield than government stocks because they are not as secure

- **Return:** Any income and/or capital gain on an investment

- **Risk:** The chance of making a loss

- **Risk appetite:** The extent to which an investor is prepared to take on risks

- **Sight bill:** Bill of exchange payable on demand

- **Term bill:** Bill of exchange payable at some future date

- **Treasury bill:** Government short-term debt, maturing in less than one year, and generally issued at a discount

Test your learning

1   **Use the picklists to complete the following sentence:**

A dividend from an investment is an example of [revenue/capital] return and an increase in the value of an investment is an example of [revenue/capital] return.

2   Government securities are also known as gilt-edged securities. They offer a variable interest rate, and are deemed low risk.

True or false?

3   **If there is a general rise in interest rates, what effect is this likely to have on the price of gilt-edged securities?**

Tick the correct answer.

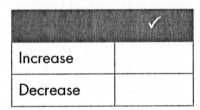

	✓
Increase	
Decrease	

4   'An unconditional order in writing from one person to another requiring the person to whom it is addressed to pay a specified sum of money, either on demand or at some future date.'

What sort of investment is this a description of?

	✓
Gilt-edged security	
Bill of exchange	
Certificate of deposit	
Local authority loan	

5   A bank pays interest of £500 every six months on a £50,000 term deposit but there is a penalty of 1% capital invested if the deposit is cashed in before the end of two years.

What rate of return will a business earn if it cashes in the deposit after holding it for just over 12 months?

| | %
|---|

6   **The 'trade-off' between risk and return is commonly used when discussing investments. Explain the meaning of this in terms of investment and borrowing.**

7 **Explain how economic factors can affect the business environment experienced by a company, especially with reference to its ability to trade.**

8 The interest yield on 7.9% treasury stock 20X5 is 6.55%. **What is the current market price?**

9 A company purchased £1,000,000 nominal value of 4% treasury stock 20X5 at a price of £117.50. The nominal value of the gilt is £100. **Calculate the total price the company paid for the gilts and the interest yield (to two dp) on the gilts.**

10 A company borrows £150,000 at a flat rate of interest of 5% per annum above base rate on the initial loan and set-up costs are 0.65% of the initial loan. The term of the loan is 24 months and the current base rate is 0.5%. **Calculate the total cost of the loan (in £).**

Activity answers

CHAPTER 1 Cash flow and profit

Activity 1: Differences between cash flow and profit

(a) Cash may be obtained from a transaction which has nothing to do with profit or loss. For example, an increase in bank overdraft provides a source of cash for payments, but it is not reported in the profit and loss account.

(b) Cash may be paid for the purchase of non-current assets, but the charge in the profit and loss account is depreciation which is only part of an asset's cost.

(c) The profit and loss account reports the total value of sales in a year. If goods are sold on credit, the cash receipts will differ from the value of sales.

(d) Similarly, the profit and loss account reports the cost of goods sold during the year. However, if materials are bought on credit, the cash payments to suppliers will be different from the value of materials purchased.

Activity 2: Cash flow from statement of profit or loss and statement of financial position

	Workings	£
Profit from operations		350,000
Change in inventory	12,000 – 21,000	(9,000)
Change in trade receivables	15,000 – 24,000	(9,000)
Change in trade payables	11,000 – 14,000	3,000
Rent prepayment		(3,500)
Electricity accrual		1,500
Depreciation charge		50,000
Loss on sale of lorry		1,700
Tax paid	65,000 + 70,000 – 75,000	(60,000)
Purchase of non-current assets	(300,000 – 50,000) – 280,000	(30,000)
NET change in cash position		294,700
Forecast cash position on 1 January 20X4		(5,000)
Forecast cash position on 31 December 20X4		289,700

Activity 3: Benje

	Workings	£
Sales receipts	8,648 + 72,960 – 6,560	75,048
Purchases payments	304 + 10,944 – 450	10,798

Activity 4: Cash on disposal of non-current assets

	✓
£21,500	
£56,500	
£70,000	
£91,500	✓

Working

Original cost	£105,000
Accumulated depreciation	– £48,500
Carrying value	£56,500
Profit on disposal	+ £35,000
Cash received on disposal of building	= £91,500

CHAPTER 2 Forecasting income and expenditure

Activity 1: Trend analysis

Average monthly sales change $= \dfrac{\text{Sales in final month} - \text{sales in first month}}{\text{Number of months} - 1}$

$$= \frac{7,200 - 5,000}{6 - 1 \text{ steps}}$$

$$= 440 \text{ units}$$

If we assume that this average increase will continue, forecast sales for July would be 7,200 + 440 = 7,640 units.

Activity 2: Regression line

Regression line: Y = 1.998 + 0.006 X

For November 20X4: X = 11 so Y = 1.998 + (0.006 ×11) = £2.064

For December 20X4: X = 12 so Y = 1.998 + (0.006 × 12) = £2.070

For January 20X5: X = 13 so Y = 1.998 + (0.006 × 13) = £2.076

Activity 3: Time series – additive model

(a)

Week	Day	Time series (TS)	Moving average = Trend (T)	Seasonal variation (SV) (TS – T)
1	Mon	600		
	Wed	1,380	930	450
	Fri	810	960	–150
2	Mon	690	990	–300
	Wed	1,470	1,020	450
	Fri	900	1,050	–150
3	Mon	780	1,080	–300
	Wed	1,560	1,110	450
	Fri	990		

Trend = This goes from 930 to 1,110 in 6 steps, ie an average of ((1,110 – 930)/6) = 30 per period.

Forecast sales

		Forecast trend	SV	Forecast sales
Week 3	Fri	1,110 + 30 = 1,140		
Week 4	Mon	1,140 + 30 = 1,170	–300	870
	Wed	1,170 + 30 = 1,200	+450	1,650
	Fri	1,200 + 30 = 1,230	–150	1,080

(b) Cash receipts in week 4 $\quad= (870 + 1,650 + 1,080) \times £1.50$

$\qquad\qquad\qquad\qquad\qquad= £5,400$

Activity 4: Time series – multiplicative model

20X4	Forecast trend £	Seasonal variation %	Forecast sales £
Q1	490,300	97	475,591
Q2	496,100	139	689,579
Q3	501,900	64	321,216
Q4	501,700	100	507,700

Activity 5: Inflation

	Workings	£
Sales		
January	(3,500 × £20)	70,000
February	(4,100 × £20 × 1.05)	86,100
March	$(4,000 \times £20 \times 1.05^2)$	88,200
Wages		
January	(3,600 × 3 hrs × £7)	75,600
February	(3,900 × 3 hrs × £7)	81,900
March	(4,200 × 3 hrs × £7 × 1.025)	90,405

Activity 6: Index numbers

(a) June 20X7 = $\dfrac{4.95}{4.8} \times 100 = 103.125$

Nov 20X7 = $\dfrac{5.1}{4.8} \times 100 = 106.25$

(b) $£4.80 \times \dfrac{108.25}{100} = £5.20$

(c) $\dfrac{108.25 - 100}{100} = 8.25\%$

Activity 7: Retail Price Index

	Workings	Overheads £
January	35,000 × 155.2/154.8 =	35,090.44
February	35,000 × 156.1/154.8 =	35,293.93

Activity 8: Mark-ups and margins

(a)

	January £	February £	March £
Purchases	32,000	24,000	28,000
Cash sales – Purchases × 140%	44,800	33,600	39,200

(b) If the mark-up on cost is 40%, then % margin on sales (to 0 dp) is **29%**.

ie (44,800 – 32,000)/44,800 × 100 = 28.57% rounded to 29%

CHAPTER 3 Patterns of cash flows

Activity 1: Types of cash flow

(a) Operational   –   Derived from normal trading operations

eg cash from sales, payments to suppliers, wages and salaries, payment for expenses

(b) Capital   –   Cash flows related to an organisation's non-current assets or its long-term funding

Outflow is the purchase of non-current assets; inflow is the proceeds from disposal of non-current assets

(c) Exceptional   –   Not expected to recur on a regular basis

eg cash from issue of new shares or the repayment of a long-term loan

Activity 2: Lagged receipts

	January £	February £	March £
Cash received from invoices issued in:			
January	0	75% × 125,000 = 93,750	125,000 – 93,750 = 31,250
February	0	0	75% × 150,000 = 112,500
March	0	0	0
Total receipts from sales	0	93,750	143,750

Activity 3: Effect of discounts on receipts

	January £	February £	March £
Cash sales (40%)	4,000	4,800	6,000
Credit sales			
Pay in same month (25% × 60% × 95% of sales)	1,425	1,710	2,137
Pay in next month (75% × 60% of sales)	4,500	4,500	5,400
Cash received	9,925	11,010	13,537

Activity 4: Lagged payments

	January £	February £	March £
Payments for purchases	45,000	0	65,000

Activity 1: St John's cash budget

	January £	February £	March £
Cash receipts:			
From opening receivables (W1)	31,480		
January invoices (W2)	115,000	69,000	46,000
February invoices (W3)		10,000	6,000
March invoices (W4)			15,000
Shop sales		400	400
Total receipts	146,480	79,400	67,400
Cash payments:			
Salaries (W5)	36,050	36,050	36,050
Repairs and maintenance	6,000	6,000	10,000
College supplies	6,300	16,500	16,500
Administration costs (W6)	17,716	17,716	17,716
Costs of stationery sales		280	280
Capital expenditure			240,000
Total payments	66,066	76,546	320,546
Net cash flow (receipts – payments)	80,414	2,854	(253,146)
Opening balance (b/f)	13,230	93,644	96,498
Closing balance (c/f)	93,644	96,498	(156,648)

Workings

1   Opening receivables = 25,250 + 3,250 + 2,980 = 31,480

2   January invoices = 184 × 1,250 = 230,000

   January: 50% × 230,000 = 115,000

   February: 30% × 230,000 = 69,000

   March: 20% × 230,000 = 46,000

3   February: 50% × 20,000 = 10,000

   March: 30% × 20,000 = 6,000

4   50% × 30,000 = 15,000

5   35,000 × 1.03 = 36,050

6   17,200 × 1.03 = 17,716

Activity 2: Bank interest in cash budget

	January £	February £	March £
Receipts before interest	13,000	15,500	16,100
Interest received @ 0.2%	11,000 × 0.2% = 22	2,422 × 0.2% = 5	0
Total receipts	13,022	15,505	16,100
Payments before interest	21,600	19,500	17,600
Interest paid @ 0.75%	0	0	1,573 × 0.75% = 12
Total payments	21,600	19,500	17,612
Net cash flow (receipts – payments)	(8,578)	(3,995)	(1,512)
Opening balance (b/f)	11,000	2,422	(1,573)
Closing balance (c/f)	2,422	(1,573)	(3,085)

Activity 3: St John's cash budget – revised

	January £	February £	March £
Cash receipts:			
From opening receivables	31,480		
January invoices (W1)	138,000	82,800	55,200
February invoices		10,000	6,000
March invoices			15,000
Shop sales		400	400
Total receipts	**169,480**	**93,200**	**76,600**
Cash payments:			
Salaries (W2)	36,400	36,400	36,400
Repairs and maintenance	6,000	6,000	10,000
College supplies	6,300	16,500	16,500
Administration costs (W3)	17,888	17,888	17,888
Costs of stationery sales		280	280
Capital expenditure			240,000
Total payments	**66,588**	**77,068**	**321,068**
Net cash flow (receipts – payments)	**102,892**	**16,132**	**–244,468**
Opening balance (b/f)	13,230	**116,122**	**132,254**
Closing balance (c/f)	**116,122**	**132,254**	**–112,214**

Workings

1   January invoices = 184 × 1,250 × 1.2 = 276,000

     January: 50% × 276,000 = 138,000

     February: 30% × 276,000 = 82,800

     March: 20% × 276,000 = 55,200

2   Salaries = 35,000 × 1.04 = 36,400

3   Administration costs = 17,200 × 1.04 = 17,888

Activity 4: Drax

(a) Revenue in pounds at the current exchange rate

€35m/1.376 = **£25,436,047**

(b) If the pound is 5% stronger:

1.376 × 1.05 = 1.4448
€35m/1.4448 = £24,224,806
This is a **decrease** of £24,224,806 – £25,436,047 = **(£1,211,241)**

(c) If the pound is 5% weaker:

1.376 × 0.95 = 1.3072
€35m/1.3072 = £26,774,786
This is an **increase** of £26,774,786 – £25,436,047 = **£1,338,739**

(d) An increase in the value of the pound.

A stronger pound means that the euro is weaker; this is **bad news for an exporter** because it means that their revenue (here in euros) will be worth less in pounds.

CHAPTER 5 Monitoring cash flows

Activity 1: Cash flow variances

	Actual cash 3-month total £	Forecast cash 3-month total £	Variance £
Cash received from invoices issued in:			
September	66,750	92,000	25,250 A
October	16,750	30,000	13,250 A
November	8,020	9,600	1,580 A
Salaries	(105,000)	(105,000)	0
Repairs and maintenance	(15,410)	(6,200)	9,210 A
College supplies	(39,930)	(39,000)	930 A
Administration costs	(51,350)	(51,000)	350 A
Dividend	(50,000)	0	50,000 A
Capital expenditure	(60,000)	(60,000)	0
Movement for 3 months	(230,170)	(129,600)	
Cash b/f	243,400	243,400	
Cash c/f	13,230	113,800	100,570 A

Activity 2: Reconciling cash flows

	£
Budgeted cash balance at 31 December 20X4	113,800
Shortfall in invoice receipts	(40,080)
Increase in repairs and maintenance expenditure	(9,210)
Increase in college supplies	(930)
Increase in administration expenditure	(350)
Unbudgeted dividend	(50,000)
Actual cash balance at 31 December 20X4	13,230

Activity 3: Causes of variances

Cause of variance	Possible actions
Delayed receipts from credit sales	• Improve credit control • Offer cash discounts for prompt payment
Reduced sales volumes	• Make improvements to product • Improve marketing • Reduce selling price
Increased volume of purchases	• Reduce wastage • Train labour • Improve stock control
Increased purchase prices	• Change suppliers • Improve negotiation with suppliers • Use cheaper materials
Payments made too soon	• Negotiate longer credit terms • Ensure full credit period is being taken
Increased labour costs	• Increase labour efficiency eg by training, less absenteeism • Reduce overtime working • Renegotiate labour contracts

Activity 4: Significant deviations and control action

(1) A shortfall in receipts from invoiced sales

Credit control and collection procedures could have been improved.

(2) Repairs and maintenance expenditure was understated

Given the extent of this expenditure, consideration could have been given to obtaining credit terms from suppliers of goods for repair and maintenance. It appears that this expenditure is paid for in the month in which it is incurred.

(3) No allowance was made for payment of the dividend

This may have been a budgeting error. Consideration could have been given to either waiving or deferring payment of the dividend in order to improve cash flow.

Activity 1: Liquid and non-liquid assets

	Liquid assets	Non-liquid assets
Notes and coins	✓	
Receivables	✓	
Property		✓
Inventory		✓
Bank balance	✓	
Short-term investments	✓	

The liquidity of receivables and inventory is variable; they cannot always be converted quickly to cash.

Activity 2: Motives for holding cash

- Transactions motive – cash is needed in order to purchase goods and to pay for any expenses incurred.

- Precautionary motive – a buffer cash balance may be required to allow for uncertainty in cash flow predictions when cash may be needed unexpectedly.

- Speculative motive – cash may be held so that any unforeseen profit-making opportunities which arise can be taken advantage of.

Activity 3: Working capital objectives

(a) Profits

Higher levels of inventory mean greater availability and possibly more choice to the customer of different variants of the product and therefore, higher sales and higher profits. Higher receivables may mean better payment terms, which may lead to higher sales and this again may lead to higher profits.

(b) Liquidity

Higher inventory and higher receivables mean more cash tied up in the short term which may lead to cash flow problems. There is sometimes a conflict between these two objectives.

Activity 4: Cash operating cycle

Average collection period	$\dfrac{172,800}{864,000}$	× 365	= 73.0 days
Inventory days	$\dfrac{270,000}{756,000}$	× 365	= 130.4 days
Average payables period	$\dfrac{86,400}{518,400}$	× 365	= 60.8 days
Cash operating cycle =			142.6 days

Activity 5: Over-capitalisation

Too much inventory – spoilage, obsolescence, storage costs

High level of receivables – greater risk of bad debt, high interest charges if there is a lack of cash so need to borrow funds

High level of cash – lost opportunity to make greater profits from better use of funds

Activity 6: Private and public sector cash management

	✓
Private sector is regulated by the Companies Act so any surplus cash can be invested as directors and shareholders wish, providing it is legal.	✓
Private sector is regulated by the Companies Act, so any surplus cash can be invested as all stakeholders wish, providing it is legal.	
Public sector is funded through public money and therefore money is only allocated where required. Any surplus should only be invested in schemes approved by central government.	✓
Public sector is funded through public money and therefore money is only allocated where required. Any surplus must be returned back to the taxpayers through tax breaks and tax cuts.	

Activity 7: Centralised treasury function

The advantages of having a centralised treasury function include:

- Centralised liquidity management avoids having a mix of cash surpluses and overdrafts in different localised bank accounts.

- Larger volumes of cash are available to invest, so better rates can be negotiated.

- Borrowing can be arranged in bulk at lower interest rates than for smaller borrowings.

- A centralised pool of buffer funds will be smaller than the sum of the separate buffer funds that would be held by the individual operations.

- A separate team will be able to monitor performance of the function more effectively.

185

Activity 1: Sources of short-term finance

Features and advantages of different forms of bank borrowing:

(a) Bank loan

Features	Advantages
• A loan is for a fixed amount, for an agreed period of time on pre-arranged terms. • It will normally be taken out with formal documentation.	• Both the customer and the bank know exactly what the repayments of the loan will be and how much interest is payable, and when. This makes planning (budgeting) simpler. • The customer does not have to worry about the bank deciding to reduce or withdraw a loan facility before he is in a position to repay what is owed. There is an element of security in being able to arrange a loan for an agreed term. • Medium-term loans normally carry a facility letter, setting out the precise terms of the agreement.

(b) Overdraft facility

Features	Advantages
• An arrangement which allows the customer to borrow money on a current account up to a specified limit. • Interest is calculated on a daily basis and charged at an agreed rate, usually a fixed percentage above the bank's base rate. • An overdraft facility is agreed for a certain time period. • Business overdrafts are usually secured eg carry a charge on business or personal assets or a personal guarantee. • An initial commitment fee may be charged for the granting of the overdraft facility.	• The customer only pays interest when the account is overdrawn. • The bank has the flexibility to review the customer's overdraft facility periodically, and perhaps agree to additional facilities, or insist on a reduction in the facility. • An overdraft can do the same job as a medium-term loan: a facility can simply be renewed every time it comes up for a review.

Features	Advantages
• Technically, an overdraft is repayable on demand to the bank. However, in practice, it would be rare for a bank to enforce this.	

Activity 2: Simple flat interest rates

	Workings	£
Total repayments	36 × £2,540	91,440
Total interest cost	£91,440 – £72,000	19,440
Interest cost p.a.	£19,440 / 3 years	6,480
Simple annual interest rate (%)	£6,480 / £72,000	9%

Activity 3: Facility letter

		Explanation
(a)	Term of the loan	The period of the loan can be tailored to the expected life of the asset.
(b)	Interest rate • Fixed • Variable • Capped	Interest rates can be fixed for the period of the loan which helps financial planning. A variable rate is set at a fixed percentage above the bank base lending rate. Usually cheaper than fixed rate but there is the risk that interest rates will rise during period of loan. With a capped rate, the bank guarantees a maximum rate of interest.
(c)	Repayment structure	Repayments can be made monthly, quarterly or annually. A repayment holiday can be arranged if there is a delay before the asset starts generating revenue.

	Explanation
(d) Any security required for the loan	
• **Personal guarantee**	Often a sole trader or partners in a partnership will be required to give personal guarantees for the money loaned. This means that, should the business fail to make payments when due, the individual guarantor will be required to pay from personal assets.
• **Fixed charge**	Security is a specific asset or group of assets which the business cannot sell during the term of the loan without the bank's permission. If the business defaults on the loan, then the bank can sell the asset in order to repay the outstanding amount.
• **Floating charge**	A charge on a certain group of assets of the business, such as receivables or inventory, which will be constantly changing. If the business defaults on the loan, then the bank has the right to be repaid from the proceeds of the pledged assets.
(e) Covenants attached to the loan	Obligations or restrictions on the business. For example: • Agreement by the business to take out no further loans until this one has been repaid • Provide regular management accounts and cash flow forecasts to the bank during the term of the loan Total loans must not exceed a set percentage of its capital employed during the term of the loan.

Activity 4: Financing options

(a) Table evaluating the best financing option:

	Arrangement fee £	Total loan interest over 5 years £	Total overdraft interest over 5 years £	Total cost of servicing finance over 5 years £	Capital repayments required £
Option 1	350	5,600 Y1 4,480 Y2 3,360 Y3 2,240 Y4 1,120 Y5 = 16,800	nil	17,150	14,000 p.a.
Option 2	nil	3,750 p.a. × 5 = 18,750	nil	18,750	When funds available
Option 3	500	3,500 p.a. × 5 = 17,500	1,000 p.a. × 5 = 5,000	23,000	50,000 at end of year 5

(b) Decision:

Option [1] (1/2/3) should be selected because:

	✓
It is the only option that complies with the partnership finance policy	✓
It is the quickest and easiest way to raise the finance	
It is the cheapest in terms of overall servicing cost	✓
The partnership will have sufficient funds to make the capital repayments needed	✓

CHAPTER 8 Managing surplus funds

Activity 1: Investment types

	Short term or long term?	Explanation
Certificates of deposit	Short term (usually six months)	• Document issued by a bank or building society which certifies that a certain sum, usually a minimum of £50,000, has been deposited with it to be repaid on a specific date • Negotiable instruments ie can be bought and sold • Offer a good rate of interest, highly marketable and can be liquidated at any time at the current market rate • Market in CDs is large and active, therefore they are an ideal method for investing large cash surpluses
Government securities:		
• Treasury bills	Short term (three months)	• Backed by government, so very low risk • Sold to banks and dealing institutions at a discount • Lowest rate of interest
• Gilts	Long term	• Mostly at a fixed interest rate and fixed period eg Treasury 5% 2019 • Can be bought and sold • The price of a gilt is affected by its coupon rate and length of time to redemption • Interest yield and redemption yield indicate return on gilts
Local authority deposits	Shorter term	• Short-term loans made to local authorities • Low risk government investment, so lower return
Shares	Long term	• Bought and sold on stock market • Aim is to get dividend and/or capital gain • Risky

Activity 2: Investing surplus funds

DogsRus needs to consider three key aspects when deciding how to invest the £60,000 of surplus funds.

Risk is the chance that the investment will fall in value and the business will make a loss. For example, shares would be far too risky.

The **return** on the investment comes from income in the form of dividend or interest or a capital gain. The higher the risk, the higher the return expected.

Liquidity is the ease and speed with which the investment can be converted into cash. DogsRus will need to pay a VAT bill next month so any investment will have to be very liquid.

The best form of investment is therefore low risk and very liquid such as a bank deposit.

Activity 3: Evaluating investment options

(a)

Investment policy criteria	Risk High/Med/Low	Within investment limit Yes/No	Annual return %	Liquidity acceptable (1 month conversion) Yes/No
Option 1	Medium	No	3.9%	Yes
Option 2	Low	Yes	3.0%	Yes
Option 3	Low	Yes	3.5%	Yes
Option 4	High	Yes	4.5%	Yes

Note. As gilts are readily marketable securities, they should be convertible into cash within one month.

(b)

	Recommended option (insert number)	Amount invested £	Total return £
Preferred option	3	50,000	1,750
Next best option	2	50,000	1,500
Total		100,000	3,250

(c) Overall the company will earn a ⟨ 3.25 ⟩ % return on its investment.

Working: 3,250/100,000 = 3.25%

Test your learning: answers

Chapter 1 Cash flow and profit

1   Although it is important for a business to **make a profit**, it can be argued that it is even more important for a business to **have a healthy cash balance** in order to be able to pay amounts when they are due.

2

	✓
Prepayment of rent	✓
Purchase of a non-current asset	✓
Purchases of inventory for cash	
Depreciation	✓
Cash sales	

3   Opening carrying amount of £275,000, less depreciation charge for year of £17,250, plus new additions = closing carrying amount of £305,000. Therefore, additions in the year must be 305,000 – 275,000 + 17,250 = £47,250.

4   On disposal, the carrying amount of the machine is its cost, less accumulated depreciation, so £55,000 – £32,500 = £22,500. However, the machine is sold for a loss of £3,750, which means the cash proceeds must be less than its carrying amount at disposal. It has therefore been sold for £22,500 – £3,750 = £18,750.

5

	£
Sales receipts 720,000 + 60,000 – 75,000	705,000
Purchases payments 471,000 + 70,000 – 104,000	437,000
Expenses payments 130,000 + 5,000 – 13,000 – 64,000	58,000
Depreciation (non-cash expense)	0

6

Purchases ledger control account

	Debit £		Credit £
		Balance b/d	24,530
Cash paid (β)	259,927		
(277,894 – 17,967)			
		Purchases	253,364
Balance c/d	17,967		
	277,894		277,894

7

Insurance expense account

	Debit £		Credit £
		Balance b/d	4,530
Cash paid (β)	14,097	Expense from statement of profit and loss	13,364
(17,894 – 3,797)			
Balance c/d	3,797		
	17,894		17,894

Chapter 2 Forecasting income and expenditure

1

		Takings £	5-day moving average £
Week 1	Tuesday	560	
	Wednesday	600	
	Thursday	630	720
	Friday	880	716
	Saturday	930	714
Week 2	Tuesday	540	716
	Wednesday	590	710
	Thursday	640	712
	Friday	850	714
	Saturday	940	708
Week 3	Tuesday	550	700
	Wednesday	560	704
	Thursday	600	710
	Friday	870	
	Saturday	970	

2 (a)

		Production in units	Trend in units
Week 1	Monday	1,400	
	Tuesday	1,600	
	Wednesday	1,800	1,630
	Thursday	1,800	1,626
	Friday	1,550	1,630
Week 2	Monday	1,380	1,636
	Tuesday	1,620	1,638
	Wednesday	1,830	1,628
	Thursday	1,810	1,642
	Friday	1,500	1,648
Week 3	Monday	1,450	1,652
	Tuesday	1,650	1,658
	Wednesday	1,850	1,672
	Thursday	1,840	
	Friday	1,570	

(b)

Increase in trend 1,672 – 1,630	=	42
Number of increases	=	10
Average increase	=	4.2 units per day

(c)

Day	Working: Trend in units	Trend in units	Seasonal variation	Forecast volume in units
Monday	1,672 + (3 × 4.2)*	1,684.6	−234.6	**1,450**
Tuesday	1,672 + (4 × 4.2)	1,688.8	−13.8	**1,675**
Wednesday	1,672 + (5 × 4.2)	1,693.0	+188	**1,881**
Thursday	1,672 + (6 × 4.2)	1,697.2	+177.8	**1,875**
Friday	1,672 + (7 × 4.2)	1,701.4	−117.4	**1,584**

* Note that the trend needs to be projected from the Wednesday of Week 3 to the Monday of Week 4, hence the need to increase by three lots of 4.2.

(d)

Total production = 1,450 + 1,675 + 1,881 + 1,875 + 1,584

= 8,465 units

Labour cost = 8,465 × 0.5 hours @ £8 = £33,860 which will be paid on the Friday of Week 4.

3

	Sales in units	Price per unit £	Cash inflow £	Purchases in units	Price per unit £	Cash outflow £
Jan	4,800	35	**168,000**	5,200	20	**104,000**
Feb	5,000	35 × 1.08	**189,000**	5,800	20 × 1.05	**121,800**
Mar	5,600	35 × 1.08	**211,680**	5,500	20 × 1.05	**115,500**

4

	✓
£162,800	
£165,600	
£168,548	
£165,649	✓

Working:

December cash payment is November overheads.

November overheads £160,000 × 1.0175 × 1.0175 = £165,649

5

	Index calculation	Expected price £
October	£10.80 × 151.6/148.5	11.03
November	£10.80 × 154.2/148.5	11.21
December	£10.80 × 158.7/148.5	11.54

6 **(a) Quarterly sales**

	Working	£
October sales	(80,000 × 160%)	128,000
November sales	(97,000 × 160%)	155,200
December sales	(78,000 × 160%)	124,800

(b)

	✓
£124,800	
£130,880	
£149,120	✓
£155,200	

Working:

	Working	£
November sales	155,200 × 80%	124,160
December sales	124,800 × 20%	24,960
Cash received		149,120

Chapter 3 Patterns of cash flows

1 Forecast cash receipts

Note that as 5% of sales are now irrecoverable debts, the timing becomes 10% cash sales, 40% month after sale, 45% two months after, 5% irrecoverable debts.

	Working	January £	February £	March £
Cash sales	10% of sales	70,000	73,000	76,000
Credit sales	720,000 × 40%	288,000		
	700,000 × 40%		280,000	
	730,000 × 40%			292,000
	750,000 × 45%	337,500		
	720,000 × 45%		324,000	
	700,000 × 45%			315,000
Total receipts from sales		**695,500**	**677,000**	**683,000**

2 Forecast cash payments

	Working	January £	February £	March £	Closing trade payables £
October purchases	592,500 × 15%	88,875			0
November purchases	562,500 × 65%	365,625			
	562,500 × 15%		84,375		0
December purchases	540,000 × 20% × 98%	105,840			
	540,000 × 65%		351,000		
	540,000 × 15%			81,000	0
January purchases	525,000 × 20% × 98%		102,900		
	525,000 × 65%			341,250	
	525,000 × 15%				78,750
February purchases	547,500 × 20% × 98%			107,310	
	547,500 × 80%				438,000
March purchases	570,000 × 100%				570,000
Total payments for purchases/ trade payables at 31 March		**560,340**	**538,275**	**529,560**	**1,086,750**

BPP
LEARNING MEDIA

Chapter 4 Preparing cash budgets

1 **(a)** **Sales receipts**

	October £	November £	December £
September sales 360,000 × 80%	288,000		
October sales 400,000 × 20% × 95%	76,000		
October sales 400,000 × 80%		320,000	
November sales 450,000 × 20% × 95%		85,500	
November sales 450,000 × 80%			360,000
December sales 460,000 × 20% × 95%			87,400
Total receipts from sales	**364,000**	**405,500**	**447,400**

(b) **Purchase payments**

	October £	November £	December £
August purchases 200,000 × 70%	140,000		
September purchases 220,000 × 30%	66,000		
September purchases 220,000 × 70%		154,000	
October purchases 240,000 × 30%		72,000	
October purchases 240,000 × 70%			168,000
November purchases 270,000 × 30%			81,000
Total payments for purchases	**206,000**	**226,000**	**249,000**

(c) General overheads

	October £	November £	December £
September overheads (30,000 – 5,000) × 20%	5,000		
October overheads (30,000 – 5,000) × 80%	20,000		
October overheads (30,000 – 5,000) × 20%		5,000	
November overheads (36,000 – 5,000) × 80%		24,800	
November overheads (36,000 – 5,000) × 20%			6,200
December overheads (36,000 – 5,000) × 80%			24,800
Total payment for overheads	**25,000**	**29,800**	**31,000**

(d) Cash budget for the quarter ending 31 December

	October £	November £	December £
Cash receipts			
Sales proceeds from equipment		4,000	
Receipts from sales	364,000	405,500	447,400
Total receipts	**364,000**	**409,500**	**447,400**
Cash payments:			
Payments for purchases	(206,000)	(226,000)	(249,000)
Wages	(42,000)	(42,000)	(42,000)
General overheads	(25,000)	(29,800)	(31,000)
Selling expenses	(18,000)	(20,000)	(22,500)
New equipment	0	(40,000)	0
Overdraft interest	(500)	0	0
Total payments	**(291,500)**	**(357,800)**	**(344,500)**
Net cash flow	**72,500**	**51,700**	**102,900**
Opening balance	**(50,000)**	**22,500**	**74,200**
Closing balance	**22,500**	**74,200**	**177,100**

2 (a) Sales receipts

	October £	November £	December £
August sales 7,000 × £60 × 40%	168,000		
September sales 7,200 × £60 × 60%	259,200		
September sales 7,200 × £60 × 40%		172,800	
October sales 6,800 × £60 × 60%		244,800	
October sales 6,800 × £60 × 40%			163,200
November sales 7,400 × £60 × 60%			266,400
Total receipts from sales	**427,200**	**417,600**	**429,600**

(b) Payments

	October £	November £	December £
September purchases 172,800 × 60%	103,680		
October purchases 163,200 × 40%	65,280		
October purchases 163,200 × 60%		97,920	
November purchases 178,800 × 40%		71,520	
November purchases 178,800 × 60%			107,280
December purchases 175,200 × 40%			70,080
Total payments for purchases	**168,960**	**169,440**	**177,360**

(c)   Cash budget for the quarter ending 31 December

	October £	November £	December £
Cash receipts:			
Sales	**427,200**	**417,600**	**429,600**
Cash payments:			
Purchases	(168,960)	(169,440)	(177,360)
Wages	(100,500)	(109,500)	(111,000)
Production overheads	(65,280)	(71,520)	(70,080)
General overheads	(52,000)	(52,000)	(58,000)
Total payments	**(386,740)**	**(402,460)**	**(416,440)**
Net cash flow	**40,460**	**15,140**	**13,160**
Opening balance	**20,000**	**60,460**	**75,600**
Closing balance	**60,460**	**75,600**	**88,760**

3

	Discount %	Cost of finance %	Accept?
Train fares	76	0.575	✓
Hotel room	1.042	2.466	✗
Dinner	11.76	1.151	✓

Workings

Discount

Train fares	(750 – 180) / 750 = 76%
Hotel room	(9,600 – 9,500) / 9,600 = 1.042%
Dinner	(170 – 150) / 170 = 11.76%

Cost of finance

To calculate the interest rate

15% ÷ 365 = 0.0411% per day

Train fares	14 × 0.0411% =	0.575%
Hotel room	60 × 0.0411% =	2.466%
Dinner	28 × 0.0411% =	1.151%

Chapter 5 Monitoring cash flows

1 **(a)**

	£
• Credit sales receipts	25,000 (A)
• Payments to credit suppliers	13,000 (A)
• Capital expenditure	40,000 (A)

(b) Three actions that the company could have taken to avoid using its overdraft facility include:

- Improve credit collection to speed up receipt of money from customers
- Lengthen the period of credit taken from suppliers
- Postpone the purchase of non-current assets

2 **Reconciliation of budgeted cash balance to actual cash balance**

	£
Budgeted cash balance at 31 May	45,200
Surplus in receipts from cash sales (45,000 – 43,000)	2,000
Shortfall in receipts from credit sales (256,000 – 231,000)	(25,000)
Shortfall in payments to suppliers (189,000 – 176,000)	(13,000)
Increase in overheads (44,500 – 43,200)	(1,300)
Increase in capital expenditure	(40,000)
Lower opening cash balance (53,400 – 52,100)	(1,300)
Actual cash balance	**(33,400)**

3 The following courses of action could improve the cash forecast position and keep the company within its agreed overdraft limit:

	✓
(i), (iii), (iv), (vii)	
(i), (ii), (v), (vi), (vii)	
(i), (ii), (v), (vii)	
(i), (iii), (iv), (v), (vi), (vii)	✓

Note that (ii) would not keep the company within the agreed overdraft limit.

4   Components

Arguments for a budget revision

The problem arose due to the liquidation of a supplier which is outside the control of the buyer, who is unlikely to have been aware it was going to happen. The event was outside the company's control.

Arguments against a revision

The deal with the new supplier was accepted without sufficient attempt to negotiate. This may have been a panicked reaction to the immediate problem which has increased costs. A more considered, careful approach would have achieved a better deal.

Conclusion

The budget revision should not be allowed. Although the liquidation was outside the control of the company, a better price could have been achieved.

Labour

Arguments for a revision

The decision to change the recruitment policy was outside the control of the departmental manager. The departmental manager is therefore not responsible for the extra cost.

Arguments against a revision

The organisation as a whole is in control of this decision, so the cost is controllable.

The departmental manager requested a change in recruitment, so is responsible for the extra cost involved.

The productivity increases have benefited the department involved, so it should also be charged with the costs involved.

Conclusion

This was an operational decision that the departmental manager requested and agreed to. It has had the desired effects, so no budget revision should be allowed.

Chapter 6 Liquidity management

1

	✓
30 days	
40 days	
54 days	✓
124 days	

Workings

Inventory holding period $= \dfrac{£68,000}{£593,000} \times 365 = $ 42 days

Trade receivables' collection $= \dfrac{£102,000}{£790,000} \times 365 = $ 47 days

Trade payables' payment $= \dfrac{£57,000}{£593,000} \times 365 = $ (35 days)

Cash operating cycle $= $ 54 days

2

	✓
25 days	
39 days	
46 days	✓
56 days	

Workings

	Days
Inventory holding period	21
Plus trade receivables' collection period	60
Less trade payables' payment period	(X)
Cash operating cycle	35

The trade payables' payment period in days is: 21 + 60 − 35 = 46 days.

3 The three most liquid assets that the majority of businesses have are:

- Cash in hand
- Bank current account
- Bank deposit account

4

	✓
Longer inventory holding period	✓
Taking longer to pay suppliers	
Lower investment in working capital	
Improved debt collection	

5 The three main principles are **security, liquidity, profitability**.

6

	✓
Overtrading	
Over-capitalisation	✓

7

	✓
Increase	
Decrease	✓

Gilts pay a fixed interest return. If inflation rises, then the purchasing power of the interest received is eroded.

8 The two main objectives of working capital management are to ensure the business has **sufficient liquid resources** to continue in operation and to **increase its profitability**.

Every business needs adequate **liquid resources** to maintain day to day cash flow. It needs enough to pay wages, salaries and accounts payable if it is to keep its workforce and ensure its suppliers continue to deliver to them.

Maintaining adequate working capital is not just important in the short term. Adequate liquidity is needed to ensure the **survival** of the business in the long term. Even a profitable company may fail without adequate cash flow to meet its liabilities.

On the other hand, an excessively conservative approach to working capital management, resulting in high levels of cash holdings, will **harm profits** because the opportunity to make a return on the assets tied up as cash will have been missed.

These two objectives will often **conflict** as liquid assets give the lowest returns.

9 **Overtrading**

The term overtrading is used because this condition commonly arises when a company is expanding rapidly. Because of increasing volumes of business, more cash is frequently needed to pay input costs such as wages or purchases than is currently being collected from accounts receivable. In other words, the company is overreliant on short-term finance to support its operations.

Symptoms of overtrading

The company will often run up its overdraft to the limit.

When the overdraft limit is reached, the company frequently raises funds from other expensive short-term sources, such as debt factoring or prompt payment discounts to customers.

It may be unable to pay accounts payable, wages and other payments on the due dates.

These problems are often compounded by a general lack of attention to cost control and working capital management, such as debt collection, because most management time is spent organising selling or production.

The company may delay investment in non-current assets and staff.

1

	✓
Trustee/beneficiary	✓
Principal/agent	
Mortgagor/mortgagee	
Bailor/bailee	

2

	✓
Honour the customer's cheque provided it is correctly made out and there are sufficient funds to pay the cheque	
Grant an overdraft when requested	✓
Respect the confidentiality of the customer's affairs	
Provide a statement showing the transactions on the customer's account within a reasonable period	

3 LIBOR stands for London **Inter-Bank Offered Rate**.

4

	✓
Floating charge required	
Interest charged only on amount of facility used	✓
Repayable on demand	

5

	✓
Overdraft finance	
Loan finance	✓

A medium-term loan from a bank would probably be the most appropriate source of finance for the purchase of the shares in B Ltd. Provided that the intention is to keep the shares for some time and therefore to benefit from income from those shares in that period, then the loan would match the timescale of the investment in the company and the income could be used to service the loan.

6 The three main repayment patterns of repaying a loan are:

- Bullet repayments
- Balloon repayments
- Amortising repayments

BPP
LEARNING MEDIA

7   A fixed charge is security against the **non-current assets** of a business.

8   Factoring is the administration of the client's invoicing, sales accounting and debt collection service.

This reduces the costs for the company in undertaking these tasks.

The factor provides credit protection for the client's debts, whereby the factor takes over the risk of loss from bad debts and so 'insures' the client against such losses.

This means that cash inflows are more predictable.

The factor makes payments to the client in advance of collecting the debts. This might be referred to as 'factor finance' because the factor is providing cash to the client against outstanding debts.

This means that the client's working capital cycle is improved.

9   If a company is to lower its capital gearing, it needs either to increase the value of its equity or to decrease the size of its borrowings.

Reduction of borrowing could be achieved by:

*   Repaying borrowings from operating funds (if growth is high and cash resources allow)

*   Using leases to convert owned assets into operating leases or sale and leaseback of assets, in order to release cash to redeem borrowings

*   Improved working capital management to reduce overdraft level, through reducing inventory and receivables, and increasing credit from suppliers

*   Increasing equity through issuing shares, either through a rights issue or placement of shares with financial institutions

Chapter 8 Managing surplus funds

1   A dividend from an investment is an example of **revenue** return and an increase in the value of an investment is an example of **capital** return.

2   False

Government securities are also known as gilts and they are considered low risk; however, the interest on gilts is fixed interest.

3

	✓
Increase	
Decrease	✓

4

	✓
Gilt-edged security	
Bill of exchange	✓
Certificate of deposit	
Local authority loan	

5 | 1% |

Workings

In the first year, the deposit will pay two lots of interest:

£500 × 2 = £1,000.

However, there is a penalty for cashing in the deposit early of 1% × 50,000 = £500.

So, overall the business earns £500/£50,000 = 1%.

6   The risk/return trade-off:

There is a **trade-off** between **risk and return**. Investors in riskier assets expect to be compensated for the risk. Thus, the return an investor expects on an equity investment will be higher than the return on government stocks or corporate bonds.

In the case of ordinary shares in a company, investors hope to achieve their return in the form of an increase in the share price (a capital gain) as well as from dividends. In general, the **higher the risk** of the security, the **more important is the capital gain** component of the expected yield.

In the same way, **higher-risk borrowers** must **pay higher yields** on their borrowing to compensate lenders for the greater risk involved. A bank will assess the creditworthiness of the borrower and set a rate of interest on its loan at a certain mark-up above its base rate. The higher the risk of default from the company, the higher the interest rate.

7   Economic factors:

Availability, price and quality of goods produced

If local or existing producers are able to supply the market with high-quality, competitively priced goods, then new or expanding companies will find it difficult to enter or grow in that market.

Inflation

Where a nation's inflation rate is high, producers will face increasing costs which will cause the price of their products to rise. This will make them less competitive and demand for their products is likely to fall.

Taxes, tariffs and trade measures

Taxes and tariffs increase the price of imports, making them less attractive to buy. Governments may attempt to help home producers with subsidies or import quotas.

The business cycle

Companies looking for growth require sufficient demand in the markets for their products. This is more likely to occur when the general economy is experiencing a period of growth.

8   The current market price is (7.9 / 6.55) × £100 = £120.61

9   The amount paid for the gilts = £1,000,000 / £100 × £117.50 = £1,175,000

Interest yield calculation:

Interest paid £1,000,000 × 4% = £40,000

Cost of investment = £1,175,000

Interest yield = (£40,000 / £1,175,000) × 100 = 3.40%

10 Interest = £150,000 × (5% + 0.5%) × 2 years = £16,500

Set-up cost = £150,000 × 0.65% = £975

Total cost of the loan = £16,500 + £975 = £17,475

Bibliography

Attorney General's Office (1882) Bills of Exchange Act. [Online] Available at: www.legislation.gov.uk [Accessed 11 May 2017].

Companies Act (2006). [Online] Available at: www.legislation.gov.uk [Accessed 11 May 2017].

Ministry of Justice (2010) *UK Bribery Act* [Online] Available at: www.legislation.gov.uk [Accessed 11 May 2017].

National Crime Agency (2002) *Proceeds of Crime Act* [Online] Available at: www.legislation.gov.uk [Accessed 11 May 2017].

UK Nolan Committee on Standards in Public Life (1995) *The 7 principles of public life.* [Online] Available at: www.gov.uk/government/publications/the-7-principles-of-public-life [Accessed 11 May 2017].

Index

REVIEW FORM

How have you used this Course Book?
(Tick one box only)

☐ Self study

☐ On a course_____

☐ Other _____

Why did you decide to purchase this Course Book? *(Tick one box only)*

☐ Have used BPP materials in the past

☐ Recommendation by friend/colleague

☐ Recommendation by a college lecturer

☐ Saw advertising

☐ Other _____

During the past six months do you recall seeing/receiving either of the following?
(Tick as many boxes as are relevant)

☐ Our advertisement in Accounting Technician

☐ Our Publishing Catalogue

Which (if any) aspects of our advertising do you think are useful?
(Tick as many boxes as are relevant)

☐ Prices and publication dates of new editions

☐ Information on Course Book content

☐ Details of our free online offering

☐ None of the above

Your ratings, comments and suggestions would be appreciated on the following areas of this Course Book.

	Very useful	Useful	Not useful
Chapter overviews	☐	☐	☐
Introductory section	☐	☐	☐
Quality of explanations	☐	☐	☐
Illustrations	☐	☐	☐
Chapter activities	☐	☐	☐
Test your learning	☐	☐	☐
Keywords	☐	☐	☐

	Excellent	Good	Adequate	Poor
Overall opinion of this Course Book	☐	☐	☐	☐

Do you intend to continue using BPP Products? ☐ Yes ☐ No

Please note any further comments and suggestions/errors on the reverse of this page. The BPP author of this edition can be emailed at: lmfeedback@bpp.com.

Alternatively, the Head of Programme of this edition can be emailed at: nisarahmed@bpp.com.

REVIEW FORM (continued)

TELL US WHAT YOU THINK

Please note any further comments and suggestions/errors below

REVIEW FORM (continued)

TELL US WHAT YOU THINK